BRITISH AND IRISH AUTHORS

Introductory Critical Studies

HENRY FIELDING

HENRY FIELDING

SIMON VAREY

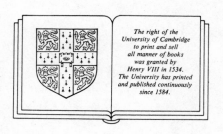

The right of the
University of Cambridge
to print and sell
all manner of books
was granted by
Henry VIII in 1534.
The University has printed
and published continuously
since 1584.

CAMBRIDGE UNIVERSITY PRESS

CAMBRIDGE

LONDON NEW YORK NEW ROCHELLE

MELBOURNE SYDNEY

Published by the Press Syndicate of the University of Cambridge
The Pitt Building, Trumpington Street, Cambridge CB2 1RP
32 East 57th Street, New York, NY 10022, USA
10 Stamford Road, Oakleigh, Melbourne 3166, Australia

© Cambridge University Press 1986

First published 1986

Printed in Great Britain at
the University Press, Cambridge

British Library cataloguing in publication data
Varey, Simon
Henry Fielding – (British and Irish authors)
1. Fielding, Henry – Criticism and
interpretation.
I. Title   II. Series
823'.5   PR3457

Library of Congress cataloguing in publication data
Varey, Simon, 1951–
Henry Fielding.
(British and Irish authors)
Bibliography
Includes index.
1. Fielding, Henry, 1707–1734 – Criticism and
interpretation.   I. Title.   II. Series.
PR3457.V37   1986   823'.5   85–28993

ISBN 0 521 26244 5 hard covers
ISBN 0 521 27876 7 paperback

Contents

Preface

This book is intended in the main for students and any other readers who would like some orientation as they come to Henry Fielding's novels. In the case of university students the study of Fielding will probably form part of a survey of eighteenth-century literature or its major novelists. Some of this book is in fact adapted from lectures I gave until recently at the University of Utrecht, as parts of precisely such courses. My criticism, like anyone else's, has its biases, but I have tried to subordinate them to the need to clarify and explain, to suggest ways of approaching Fielding rather than present packaged interpretations. It is not my purpose to parade modish critical approaches, so readers anxious to discover the feminist's Fielding, the deconstructionist's Fielding, or the neo-Marxist's Fielding, will catch at best only accidental glimpses of him here. This book is meant to introduce Fielding's major work.

Although a book of this kind is not the place for detailed historical scholarship, the literature it discusses is richer if it can be placed in its cultural and political contexts. Within the limited space available, these shape my account of Fielding's work, as they shaped his development as a versatile writer: playwright, journalist, pamphleteer, and legal essayist, as well as glamorous novelist.

The critical work listed in my bibliography to some extent reflects and influences my own writing. However, my account of Fielding is not a synthesis of modern criticism, even though it may look like that because, to save space, I have not used footnotes. Authors whose work I quote or refer to in the text (usually with a short title and page reference) are listed in my bibliography, as are some others who are not actually quoted.

A substantial portion of my manuscript, all my notes, and even some of my copies of Fielding's books were stolen in the spring of 1984 by a New York thief. When he found out the value of what he had taken, he probably cursed me as much as I cursed him. But, in circumstances which I do not recommend, I learned very quickly who my friends were. For the support that has enabled me to finish writing this book, it is my pleasure to thank Jerry and Rita Beasley, Bill and Marlene Park, Carol Varey, and Richard Varey, as well as

PREFACE

numerous others whose offers of help I never in fact took up. My thanks too to the William Andrews Clark Memorial Library, whose genial staff let me take over a computer terminal to process my words. And finally, I am very grateful to Terry Moore, of Cambridge University Press, for being such a forbearing editor.

Fielding would have approved: he used to celebrate such good nature.

Los Angeles, 1985   SIMON VAREY

A note on texts

I have quoted from the volumes published so far in the Wesleyan edition of Fielding's *Works*. Until this series has been completed, one can easily consult most of Fielding's writings in *Complete Works of Henry Fielding*, edited by W. E. Henley, 16 volumes (1903, reprinted 1967). However, because these unannotated texts were not very well edited, I prefer not to quote from them, and instead have used either first editions, or modern editions, often designed for use in classrooms, of individual works whose texts are accurate and notes helpful.

After textual accuracy, my main concern is accessibility. I have given book and chapter references from the novels, act and scene references if possible from the plays. This means that readers can usually track down quotations without much trouble even if they are using different editions. In the case of the *Journal of a Voyage to Lisbon*, which is not so conveniently divided, I have given page references to the rare 'second' edition and added references to the Everyman reprint.

In abbreviated form, these are the other editions I have used:

The Wesleyan edition for: *Miscellanies*, vol. 1 (1972); *Joseph Andrews* (1967); *Tom Jones* (1974); *Amelia* (1983).

Everyman edition for *A Journey from this World to the Next* (1973).

Penguin edition for *Jonathan Wild* (1982).

Oxford English Novels edition of *Joseph Andrews and Shamela*, for *Shamela* (1970).

Regents Restoration Drama Series for: *The Author's Farce* (1966); *The Grub-Street Opera* (1968); *The Historical Register for the Year 1736* (1967).

First editions of all Fielding's other works, unless otherwise specified.

The bibliography at the end of this book gives full details of all these editions.

1

The making of a satirist

It is difficult for us to imagine living in a world without novels. In 1707 Henry Fielding was born into a society in which the novel was not yet an established literary genre. In due course he would become a celebrated pioneer of the novel, but he lived as a writer for fourteen years before his first novel was published. After a brief foray into satirical verse, Fielding embarked on his literary career in 1728. To bring him fame and – he hoped – fortune, the aspiring young writer looked not to the novel, but to the theatre.

Plays of the late 1720s belonged in a general sense to what is still sometimes – very loosely – called Restoration drama. The comedies written and performed in Fielding's youth were usually social and domestic, often turning on amorous intrigues and the closet-door plots of farce. The tragedies were still often 'heroic', devoid of much action, with a tendency to be bombastic, and liable to celebrate the virtues of noble patriots who strive to resolve the conflict of duty and love. The major difference between the witty, cynical, and sophisticated drama of the late seventeenth century and the typical plays of the early eighteenth was the introduction after about 1700 of a sentimental strain.

Sentimental drama laid great stress on the innate virtue of human beings: thus, unbelievably virtuous maidens in situations of pitiful distress resist the seductions of rakes who miraculously reform, for 'no other Reason,' said Fielding later, 'than because the Play is drawing to a Conclusion' (*Tom Jones*, VIII. i). The two leading purveyors of sentimental comedy, Richard Steele and Colley Cibber, exploited these types of character for all they were worth: the virtuous characters are duly rewarded with a happy end-ing, brought about more often than not by a plot of stunning improbability. Tear-jerking endings therefore encourage an artificiality for which sentimental drama is notorious. The virtues of chastity and loyalty are glorified in these pathetic plays addressed largely to the audience's emotions. Such comedy stands in contrast with its predecessors of the late Restoration period: the refusal to idealise – sometimes becoming sheer cynicism – is toned down or in some way averted or just overcome by the virtuous; the bawdy is

1

frequently cleaned up; and the witty, sparkling dialogue of the best plays by Wycherley, Vanbrugh, or Congreve gives way to a greater emphasis on situation and character. As Arthur Sherbo has pointed out, if we are told often enough that a distressed maiden is virtuous, we will eventually believe that she is, without having to see much evidence of her virtue on the stage. Characters in sentimental comedy therefore can tend to be like ciphers.

Another new dramatic form that had a great impact was ballad opera. In this type of play, songs are fully integrated with spoken dialogue, so that the result is usually an entertainment rather like the modern musical. The music itself, in these plays, consists of popular ballad tunes, but with new words. The first and best-known example of ballad opera is John Gay's *Beggar's Opera*. As well as devising a new form of opera, Gay blended burlesque of Italian opera with social and political satire. Less obviously, he also burlesqued the inflated verbal style of the 'new' comedy. His extremely popular *Opera* prompted dozens of imitations in the 1730s and 1740s.

Between 1728 and 1737 Fielding turned out farces, ballad operas, sentimental comedies, and political satires. Including his major revisions of his own plays, three translations, and one lost text, Fielding wrote twenty-eight pieces for the theatre. Some are conventional five-act plays designed for a full evening's entertainment, others just brief afterpieces intended to follow a longer drama and hence round off the evening. Whatever their length or form, most of Fielding's plays are not confined to a single genre: *The Lottery* (1732), for instance, is a farce in the form of a ballad opera; and as early as 1730 political satire appeared in one of Fielding's farces, *Rape upon Rape: or, the Coffee-House Politician*. Fielding's dramatic writing was neither constantly political nor, usually, doggedly sentimental. Instead, he blended different modes, achieving his best results, it seems to me, in his burlesque farces.

Although Fielding's dramatic output was prolific, few of his plays are read now, almost none performed. London theatregoers in 1967 would know that Bernard Miles' musical, *Lock Up Your Daughters*, was freely adapted from *Rape upon Rape*. Some will recognise *Tom Thumb* as Fielding's. But many readers of the novels know that Fielding was a playwright only because they associate his name with the notorious Licensing Act of 1737, which enabled the Lord Chamberlain to have plays censored until as recently as 1968. Modern critics have not been kind to Fielding the playwright:

George Bernard Shaw was virtually alone in his provocatively extravagant praise of Fielding's drama, while the more reasoned critical approaches to the plays tend to view the earlier years of Fielding's literary career from the perspective of his later years as a novelist. The result of such approaches is that the plays are reviewed and found wanting or are merely ransacked for parallels to the novels.

The received critical opinion of Fielding's plays is that they reveal the political satirist and the potential novelist, but critical emphasis has been placed on Fielding's dramatic satires of 1731–2 and 1736–7 and on his burlesques at the cost of excluding his non-satirical plays from much serious discussion. Perhaps some of the plays are not worth discussing, but to ignore them in an outline of Fielding's growth from playwright to novelist is a mistake. Fielding in the late 1720s was not a dedicated opposition satirist, and for much of his theatrical career he appears to have been less interested in writing political satire than in writing simply for the theatre. Fielding's development as a writer is distorted if the sentimental is excluded – as it usually is – in favour of the satirical.

When Fielding's dramatic career came to an end in 1737, he published no new work for two years. The next we hear of him as a writer is his appearance in November 1739 as an editor of a newspaper, the *Champion*, to which he contributed for about eighteen months. In this chapter I shall not attempt to discuss in detail the whole body of Fielding's earlier writing. Instead, I shall seek to trace the development of his characteristic voice first during his nine years as an active playwright and then during his spell as a journalist on the *Champion*. I want to illustrate what Fielding was thinking and writing about and how he habitually expressed himself up to the time he began to conceive his first novels. Fielding did not become a novelist overnight: he brought to his prose fiction a wealth of experience, which this chapter seeks, in a limited scope, to explore.

During Fielding's first few months as a writer in London, the literary life of the city was buzzing. On 29 January 1728 *The Beggar's Opera* began a two-month run, which spectacularly broke previous box-office records, and on 18 May the first edition of Pope's *Dunciad* took the city by storm. Nor, of course, had anyone forgotten *Gulliver's Travels*, not yet two years old. Political writing had been boosted by all of these, as well as by the eminent weekly newspaper, the *Craftsman*, to which Lord Bolingbroke and William Pulteney contributed regularly. All these writers had brought satire, politics, and literature closer together, so that to a greater extent than ever before writing itself was often a political activity.

The main target of political writing, Sir Robert Walpole, had held control of the Whig government since April 1722. A patchwork of Whigs, Tories, and Jacobites made up an opposition that was more vociferous and better organised than any previously, but it was unable to remove Walpole or break his power until 1742. Walpole's efficient government depended on a system of bribery and corruption, which became the two catchwords of an infuriated opposition in Parliament and of an army of writers in the press. Although some of the attacks on the 'prime minister' (a term of near-abuse given currency by the *Craftsman*) were blatant invective, others were more subtly ironic. The opposition writers developed an allusive political vocabulary, such that 'a certain *Great Man*' invariably meant Walpole and 'patriotism' meant 'opposition'. The writers on the opposition side were certainly more illustrious than those who wrote in defence of Walpole's administration. Although in William Arnall the ministry had a gifted journalist and in Lord Hervey an eloquent and effective occasional writer, the opposition had all the glamour.

A young man wishing to penetrate this literary milieu could try for patronage from the court or he could publish 'opposition' satire, which might bring him notoriety and a little money and might even encourage the court to buy his silence. Fielding approached his second cousin, Lady Mary Wortley Montagu, who was influential if not especially powerful at court. She was indirectly responsible – at least in part – for the political stance of one of Fielding's early attempts at verse, a burlesque epic (c. 1729) that satirised Pope, Swift, Gay, and the *Craftsman*. This undistinguished verse was left unfinished and, until 1972, unpublished. In so far as Fielding was engaged in political writing, his early allegiance lay with the court, not the opposition.

At the end of January 1728 Fielding had published his little satirical verse, *The Masquerade*, written by 'Lemuel Gulliver, Poet Laureat to the King of Lilliput' and aimed at John James Heidegger, then an impresario who was prominent in London's theatrical circles. *The Masquerade* was scarcely noticed, since the major literary event was the opening of *The Beggar's Opera*. Although this play was such a brilliant and influential triumph, the most successful playwright of the period (measured by the number of performances) was not Gay, but Cibber. Politically, Gay and Cibber were diametrically opposite: virtually overnight Gay became a spokesman for the opposition, while Cibber, thought to be already in Walpole's pay, was being portrayed in the press as analogous to Walpole, running his theatre in the same high-handed and corrupt manner as the first minister ran his government. Cibber, however, avoided politics in his plays and achieved great popularity with a succession of sentimental comedies. Indeed, with one of them, *The Provok'd Husband*, running at Drury Lane since 10 January and *The Beggar's Opera* monopolising Lincoln's Inn Fields, Fielding's entrance into London's theatrical world was delayed several weeks.

On 16 February 1728 Fielding's first play, *Love in Several Masques*, was produced at the Theatre Royal in Drury Lane. Lady Mary lent a helping hand here too: Fielding dedicated to her 'this slight Work', which 'arose from a Vanity, to which your Indulgence, on the first Perusal of it, gave Birth' (iii–iv). Furthermore, she went to see it twice. Fielding covered himself against possible failure by drawing attention apologetically to his youth and inexperience, but he scarcely needed to do so. 'Slight Work' though it is, *Love in Several Masques* is an agreeable light comedy that enjoyed modest success. Following the dramatic conventions of the day, Fielding devised characters with self-explanatory names, such as Merital, Malvil, Lord Formal, Lady Matchless, and Sir Positive Trap, in the tradition of the comedy of humours, where (as Ben Jonson said) 'one peculiar quality' dominates a character's temperament. Fielding's plot is a variation on a stock Restoration comic plot, in which at least two men profess love for one woman, who prefers a third, but disguises her true feelings. This scheme provides an opportunity for some mild social satire directed at the manners and customs of fashionable London society, in contrast with 'honest' but unsophisticated country ways. In its general tone and dramatic structure, the play vaguely resembles Congreve's *Love for Love*, without achieving the substance or stature of the earlier play: indeed, Fielding's first play is usually dismissed (by the few who take any notice of it at all) because it is imitation Congreve.

Fielding nods in the direction of the sentimental by having Lady Matchless change her mind and marry the honest country 'philosopher' Wisemore, so that his contempt of fortune – at odds with the received attitude of polite society – is rewarded in the end. This is rare in a world where 'Beauty is now considered as a Qualification only for a Mistress, and Fortune for a Wife', as Merital puts it (13), and 'Right is a sort of Knight-Errant whom we have long since laughed out of the World. Merit is Demerit,

Constancy Dulness, and Love an out-of-fashion *Saxon* Word which no polite Person understands', as Lady Matchless tells Wisemore (51). But Wisemore is not the stock country buffoon of this type of social comedy: he has seen London society before and has decided to reject it. He is no *ingénu*:

> I had taken leave of this place long ago, its Vanities, Hurries, and superficial, empty, ill-digested Pleasures . . . Who wou'd waste his Afternoons in a Coffee-House, or at a Tea-Table, to be entertained with Scandal, Lies, Balls, Operas, Intrigues, Fashions, Flattery, Nonsense, and that Swarm of Impertinences which compose the common place Chat of the World? Who would bear all this, did he know the Sweets of Retirement? . . . *London* is to me, what the Country is to a gay, giddy Girl, pampered up with the Love of Admiration; or a young Heir just leapt into his Estate and Chariot. It is a Mistress, whose Imperfections I have discovered, and cast off. I know it; I have been a Spectator of all its Scenes. I have seen Hypocrisy pass for Religion, Madness for Sense, Noise and Scurrility for Wit, and Riches for the whole Train of Virtues. (7)

Fielding seems never to have lost such contempt for London's high society. Wisemore's denunciation of London here involves his preference for the country over the city, a formulation that Fielding – like Pope, Swift, and Bolingbroke – adopted in *Joseph Andrews* and *Tom Jones*. The distinction between the joys of the country and the corruptions of the city often carries political implications, too, which may explain the oddity that writers who loved London should be among the first to condemn the place.

Love in Several Masques shows Fielding making use of conventions of both sentimental and satiric comedy. The satire is perhaps more conventional than felt, and anyway the dominant tone of the play is not satiric, but comic. But Fielding clearly conceived of his play as satiric comedy. Inspired by 'his Comick Muse':

> No private Character these Scenes expose,
> Our Bard, at Vice, not at the Vicious, throws.
> If any by his pointed Arrows smart,
> Why did he bear the Mark within his Heart? (1)

This assumption that only the guilty will be hurt – and deservedly – is a convention of Augustan satire. So too is the claim that the author exposes vice rather than the vicious: in fact Samuel Johnson's *Dictionary* would later define satire by noting its generality, as opposed to any reflections on individuals. Fielding was adopting a conventional posture, which had been used in the theatre by those masters of satiric comedy, Ben Jonson, John Marston, and William Congreve. Fielding was therefore joining a tradition of comedy whose purpose was to ridicule human follies and vices: in fact, some people thought that this was the *only* aim of true comedy.

In the seven plays that Fielding wrote between 1728 and 1731 the blend of the sentimental with social satire is the basis on which he builds. The heroines are incomparably virtuous and sweet-natured, while their tyrannical fathers are outwitted by scheming young sparks who marry these young ladies. These early plays develop an increasingly satirical tone. Fielding's commitment to satiric comedy emerges in most of his subsequent drama and accounts to some extent for his mixture of sentimental and satiric. Satire is almost inevitably the enemy of sentiment, as Edmund Burke (who thought true comedy was satiric) commented,

our Modern Stage Directors think Satyr the greatest Fault in a Comedy, and as they know the relish of the Town, give high Encouragement to Plays that abound with Characters insipidly perfect, where Virtue is painted in an unnatural, and consequently an unamiable manner.

(*The Reformer*, no. 10, 31 March 1748)

Thus a combination of these two opposites in a single comedy seems to imply a serious contradiction in the author's mind. When Fielding tried his hand at sentimental comedy, the results were by almost general consent accounted disastrous, but his farces and burlesques have always been held in higher esteem. One reason is that Fielding's own use of the sentimental acts as a necessary counterpoint to his satire. His own conception of satire involved its function as an agent of correction and reproach: that meant portraying evils and abuses as they really are, because, as he would say later,

we are much better and easier taught by the examples of what we are to shun, than by those which would instruct us what to pursue.

(*The Champion*, 10 June 1740)

Examples may perhaps have more Advantage than Precepts, in teaching us to avoid what is odious, than in impelling us to pursue what is amiable.

(*Covent-Garden Journal*, no. 21, 14 March 1752)

Sentimental comedy, as Fielding knew, was also intended to give an audience exemplary models of virtue and good conduct. The most extreme form of this, Steele's *Conscious Lovers*, was rarer in practice

7

than the idea was in theory. Like Swift, Fielding incorporated both kinds of example, while giving more weight to examples of what to avoid. This is as true of his dramatic satires as it is of *Jonathan Wild*, whose eponymous hero is treated satirically and whose virtuous but pathetic 'heroes', the Heartfrees, are derived from sentimental comedy. In Fielding's vision, the two opposites, virtue and vice, must meet and must clash.

Fielding signalled his gradual move towards an emphasis on the satiric in 1730 by adopting the pseudonym of 'H. Scriblerus Secundus', the supposed author of *The Author's Farce*. This choice of pseudonym imitated Martinus Scriblerus, the fictional character invented in 1713 by Pope, Swift, Gay, Arbuthnot, Parnell, and Harley, whose aim was to satirise false and misguided learning. An ingenious and unconventional parody, *The Author's Farce* bore more than passing resemblance to *The Beggar's Opera*. In *The Tragedy of Tragedies* (1731) H. Scriblerus Secundus indulged in Scriblerian satire like Swift's notes to *A Tale of a Tub* and Pope's notes to *The Dunciad*, where a supposedly learned commentator is made responsible for ludicrously inappropriate scholarly annotation of the text. Although these might seem to be signs that Fielding had thrown in his lot with the opposition satirists, his plays were still only obliquely political at this time, and the Scriblerians themselves gave no indication of any interest in him. Indeed, in the *Craftsman* of 22 August 1730, 'Courtly Grub' mentioned that Walpole notoriously 'gave no small Encouragement to those sublime Productions, *Hurlothrumbo* [a popular farce by Samuel Johnson of Cheshire] and *Tom Thumb*'.

One obvious way in which Fielding aligned himself with the Scriblerians was to incorporate a few jokes at the expense of their perpetual butt, Colley Cibber, who in 1728 had played Rattle in *Love in Several Masques* and who would continue to act in Fielding's plays. But Cibber was only one of several targets in Fielding's satire. *The Author's Farce* and *Tom Thumb* are directed mainly at pretension – something Fielding always detested – especially the pretensions of the theatre managers, and the corruptions of the whole industry of writing and publishing. The earlier of the two plays, *The Author's Farce*, contains a host of characters who are barely recognisable to most modern readers, but who originally 'took off' fairly well-known personalities. Bookweight, a bookseller (the period's nearest equivalent to a present-day publisher), runs a writing factory in which hacks are urged to write replies to their own works. Bookweight has been thought to represent Edmund Curll, but Curll was only the most notorious of the many London booksellers who indulged in such practices. If this sort of allusion seems too limited in scope and interest, let us see what Fielding can do with another stock situation, this time the theatre manager hearing a new play and advising changes to make it conform to his audience's taste. The contemporary joke was about Cibber (here represented by Marplay) and his fellow-patentee at Drury Lane, Robert Wilks (here Sparkish). The author (Luckless) could be anyone. Hearing Luckless read five lines of his play:

MARPLAY: I could alter those lines to a much better idea.
> *With thee, the barren blocks* (that is, trees)
> > *where not a bit*
> *Of human face is painted on the bark,*
> *Look green as Covent Garden in the spring.*
LUCKLESS: Green as Covent Garden?
MARPLAY: Yes, Covent Garden Market, where they sell greens.
LUCKLESS: Montrous! Sir, I must ask your pardon, I cannot consent to such an alteration. It is downright nonsense.
MARPLAY (*rising from the table*):
> Sir, it will not do, and so I would not have you think any more of it.
SPARKISH: No, no, no. It will not do.
LUCKLESS: What faults do you find?
MARPLAY: Sir, there is nothing in it that pleases me, so I am sure there is nothing in it that will please the town.
SPARKISH: There is nothing in it that will please the town.

These characters surely have more than only topical interest: the spineless Sparkish, who can only parrot the words of his more powerful partner, and the arrogant ignorance of Marplay, who says he knows his business yet who will destroy the very meaning of the play he would alter; these are not caricatures confined to the eighteenth century, but human beings we still meet today. These satirical examples are given a political dimension at the beginning of the next scene, where Marplay admits to Sparkish that the play they have rejected 'may be a very good one for aught I know' but that he cares only for 'interest', that is, political influence. The density of the topical allusions, it seems to me, does not obscure either Fielding's perception of character types or his ability to enliven stock situations with satiric verve.

The general object of Fielding's earliest satire had been the conventional one of the decay of virtue, but by April 1730 in his

best-known burlesque, *Tom Thumb*, his main satiric thrust was far
more effectively aimed at his fellow dramatists in Grub Street.
Here again there is a hint that Fielding is jumping on the
Scriblerian bandwagon, since the *Craftsman* and *The Dunciad* had
already made the political connection between government and
the theatre. The new farce was, however, the history of 'Tom
Thumb the Great', an unmistakable allusion to 'a certain great
man'.

In an age when epic and tragedy were valued as the two
highest forms of literature, no one had written either a worthwhile
epic (although Pope had just written a worthwhile mock-epic) or
a passable tragedy. It was tragedy, particularly, that Fielding
had in his sights when he wrote *Tom Thumb*. Probably the
funniest scene of the play is the last, in which the ghost of Tom
Thumb (who has been unheroically eaten by a passing cow)
appears:

GHOST: *Thom* [*sic*] *Thumb* I am – but am not eke alive.
    My Body's in the Cow, my Ghost is here.
GRIZZLE: Thanks, O ye Stars, my Vengeance is restor'd,
    Nor shalt thou fly me – for I'll kill the Ghost.
                                   (*Kills the* Ghost)
HUNCAMUNCA: O barbarous Deed – I will revenge him so.
                                 (*Kills* Grizzle)
DOODLE: Ha! *Grizzle* kill'd – then Murtheress beware.
                         (*Kills* Huncamunca)
QUEEN: O Wretch – have at thee.   (*Kills* Doodle)
NOODLE: And have at thee too.   (*Kills the* Queen)
CLEORA: Thou'st kill'd the Queen.   (*Kills* Noodle)
MUSTACHA: And thou hast kill'd my Lover. (*Kills* Cleora)
KING: Ha! Murtheress vile, take that. (*Kills* Mustacha)
    And take thou this. (*Kills himself, and falls*)

At the end of the play, therefore, there are nine deaths in about
half a minute, leaving the stage strewn with bodies, without one
character left alive. On the occasions when *Tom Thumb* is revived,
this scene is a guaranteed success. Like the best satire, *Tom Thumb*
retains its general point – to ridicule pretension – although the
specific one – to ridicule heroic tragedy – is really lost on most
of us now.

The preface to the second edition of *Tom Thumb* is important in Fielding's development in these early years. With a witty jauntiness and poker-faced irony, he defends his dramatic innovations in the original *Tom Thumb*: these included the mad parody of tragic deaths and also the killing of Tom Thumb's ghost (which he later dropped). Here is a short extract:

> Mr. *Lock* complains of confused Ideas in Words, which is entirely amended by suffering them to give none at all: This may be done by adding, diminishing, or changing a Letter, as instead of *Paraphernalia*, writing *Paraphonalia*: For a Man may turn *Greek* into Nonsense, who cannot turn Sense into either *Greek* or *Latin* . . .[1]
> And here I congratulate my Cotemporary Writers, for their having enlarged the Sphere of Tragedy: The ancient Tragedy seems to have had only two Effects on an Audience, *viz.* It either awakened Terror and Compassion, or composed those and all other uneasy Sensations, by lulling the Audience in an agreeable Slumber. But to provoke the Mirth and Laughter of the Spectators, to join the Sock to the Buskin, is a Praise only due to Modern Tragedy. (iii–iv)

Setting himself apart from modern playwrights, Fielding pushes modern tragedy over the limits of rationality and into the realm of the absurd. Once he turned to burlesque, Fielding seems to have found his most effective and entertaining mode. His parodic gifts brought him great success, while also finding him a form of satire that was at once ironic and absurd.

One celebrated example of this love of parody is his satire of a much maligned line from James Thomson's recent tragedy *Sophonisba* (1730):

> GRIZZLE: Oh! *Huncamunca, Huncamunca*, oh,
> Thy pouting Breasts, like Kettle-Drums of Brass,
> Beat everlasting loud Alarms of Joy;
> As bright as Brass they are, and oh, as hard;
> Oh *Huncamunca, Huncamunca!* oh!
> HUNCAMUNCA: Ha! do'st thou know me, Princess as I am,
> That thus of me you dare to make your Game.
> GRIZZLE: Oh *Huncamunca*, well I know that you
> A Princess are, and a King's Daughter too.
> But Love no Meanness scorns, no Grandeur fears,

---

[1] Alluding to Cibber's notoriously ignorant misspelling in the preface to *The Provok'd Husband* (1728).

11

> Love often Lords into the Cellar bears,
> And bids the sturdy Porter come up Stairs.
> For what's too high for Love, or what's too low?
> Oh *Huncamunca, Huncamunca*, oh!   (*Tragedy of Tragedies*, II. v)

Poor Thomson must have regretted ever conceiving those words, 'Oh, Sophonisba, Sophonisba, oh!' once Fielding's scene first occurred on stage. Fielding's peculiar talent here is to create incongruous images which juxtapose the lofty and the 'low'. Contemporary tragedy is thus reduced to absurdity and banality.

The play from which this parody is quoted, *The Tragedy of Tragedies* (1731), is a revised version of *Tom Thumb*. Fielding abandoned his previous preface and wrote an entirely new one, in which he introduced the fiction that he now presented to the public a newly discovered manuscript (hence the mock scholarly footnotes). The preface is as much a travesty as the play: Horace is interpreted to say 'That Bombast is the proper Language for Joy, and Doggrel for Grief'; Cicero to suggest that nothing is 'so proper for Tragedy as a Set of big sounding Words, so contrived together, as to convey no Meaning; which I shall one Day or other prove to be the Sublime of *Longinus*'. In the new play itself, even the dramatis personae is funny and parodic:

Tom Thumb the Great, A little hero with a great Soul, something violent in his Temper, which is a little abated by his Love for *Huncamunca* . . .

Queen Dollalolla, Wife to King *Arthur*, and Mother to *Huncamunca*, a Woman entirely faultless, saving that she is a little given to Drink; a little too much a *Virago* towards her Husband, and in Love with *Tom Thumb*.

The Princess *Huncamunca*, Daughter to their Majesties King *Arthur* and Queen *Dollalolla*, of a very sweet, gentle, and amorous Disposition, equally in Love with Lord *Grizzle* and *Tom Thumb*, and desirous to be married to them both.

One of Fielding's favourite jocular techniques is to qualify a compliment, such as Dollalolla's being faultless, so much that it finally comes to mean the opposite.

Whatever he chose – burlesque, farce, or sentimental comedy – by 1731 Fielding's characteristic tone was the ironic one of satiric comedy. All his plays were intended to 'reform' the age in some respect: the dramatic satires expose and ridicule the vain, the hypocritical, the greedy, and the corrupt, while the sentimental plays and scenes provide examples of virtue, integrity, and honesty to be imitated. Fielding's preference for satiric comedy did not produce a play wholly devoted to a political subject until the satirical *Welsh Opera* (1731), soon to be revised, expanded, and just as inaptly titled *The Grub-Street Opera* (1731). This revised opera begins with an 'Introduction' which imitates that of *The Beggar's Opera* and ends as Gay's play ends with the argument that the rich and poor have the same vices, but only the poor are punished for them. Such obvious association with Gay's largely political play could only be strengthened by Fielding's first extended satirical allusions to Walpole.

The Grub-Street Opera is a satirical ballad opera whose characters are all members of a single household. The head of the Welsh family, Sir Owen Apshinken, is cheated continually by his servants, whose amorous adventures provide a good deal of the action. It is, says Scriblerus, 'a sort of family opera' (vi). The family as a political metaphor was well established by this time: the opposition press was fond of portraying Walpole as a dishonest servant in the employ of the King or the British people. *The Grub-Street Opera* has been seen as a satire on the royal family, but King George and Queen Caroline, though discernible in the characters of the master of the house and his wife, are not dominant. The main target here is certainly Walpole, presented in a suitable role as Robin the butler. None could mistake the long-standing joke: 'there's cheating in his very name. – Robin, is as much as to say, robbing' (III. xiv). Robin quarrels with the coachman, William, who represents William Pulteney, leader of the Parliamentary opposition and a prominent journalist, whom Walpole had once employed in government. Other contemporary figures are here and would certainly have been recognised by an audience in 1731, had *The Grub-Street Opera* escaped the unofficial censorship of Walpole's ministry. Censorship itself confirms the play's political satire. The satirical point of the opera, like so much contemporary political satire, would have depended on an audience's applying the general satire to specific people and topical events. Hence (especially after *The Beggar's Opera*) the following air says nothing specific about Walpole, yet can legitimately be taken to apply to him. If we prefer, we can just take it as a durable general comment about the structure of society:

Great courtiers palaces contain
While small ones fear the gaol,
Great parsons riot in champagne,
Small parsons sot on ale;
Great whores in coaches gang,
Smaller misses,
For their kisses,
Are in Bridewell bang'd; [sic]
While in vogue
Lives the great rogue,
Small rogues are by dozens hang'd.   (II. v)

Derived directly from Gay, this theme reappears in Fielding's later work.

When *The Modern Husband* was performed on 14 February 1732 at Drury Lane, Fielding seemed to have recanted the heresy of writing low farce. The printed text is dedicated to Walpole, of all people: some critics therefore think the dedication must be ironic. However, *The Modern Husband* eschews politics and so effectively lives up to its prologue's promise to portray moral corruption as it is, that the play has been condemned as sordid. But Fielding still, obviously, believed that the theatre offered a medium for moral improvement as well as entertainment, or, in the contemporary cliché, 'instruction and delight'. *The Modern Husband*, a regular five-act play, is close in some ways to a fully fledged sentimental comedy, but in a major departure from the usual examples of the genre, Mr Modern – the husband of the title – sells his wife for £1,500 in order to pay off their gambling debts. One character, Lord Richly, is a more ruthless, cynical villain than any Fielding had previously created – more even than the repellent, corrupt magistrate, Squeezum, in *Rape upon Rape*. In one of the most distasteful images, Richly explains his system of using his wealth to trap women: 'I have succeeded often by leaving Money in a Lady's Hands; she spends it, is unable to pay, and then I, by Virtue of my Mortgage, immediately enter upon the Premises' (IV. ii). Clearly, he regards women as property. Where Squeezum got his just deserts, Richly does not. He is boldly confronted (something he is not used to) by the honest Bellamant, who will not mince his words when he condemns (implicitly) all the Richlys of London society:

14

No, the Language of Flatterers and hireling Sycophants has been what you have dealt in – Wretches, whose Honour and Love are as venal as their Praise. Such your Title might awe, or your Riches bribe to Silence; such you should have dealt with, and not have dared to injure a Man of Honour . . . Where Grandeur can give Licence to Oppression, the People must be Slaves, let them boast what Liberty they please. (V.vi)

But Richly's part in the drama does not end in the ignominy that this plain speaking might seem to predict. It ends instead on a face-saving but still cynical note, when he discovers that he has himself been tricked: his daughter has secretly married Bellamant's son, of all people, but he overcomes his annoyance by taking 'very little Trouble to be revenged on any of you; being heartily convinced, that in a few Months you will be so many mutual Plagues to one another' (V. xiii). Yet *The Modern Husband* does not present unrelieved gloom and corruption. In the sentimental mode the men and women of honour and virtue come through their many distresses to be properly rewarded with happiness in the end.

Later in the same year, 1732, Fielding wrote a short afterpiece, *The Covent Garden Tragedy*, to follow his new comedy, *The Old Debauchees*. Perhaps because *The Modern Husband* was not particularly well received, Fielding turned again to exaggeration and burlesque ridicule in his new afterpiece. Once more he turned high tragedy into low farce. In *The Covent Garden Tragedy* his characters are denizens of Covent Garden, thus almost by definition they are whores, bawds, and rakes, who swear oaths not by any recognised deity, but by gin, and so on. Fielding's humour is found mainly where he ridicules tragedy by burlesquing it:

CAPT. BILKUM: If born to swing, I never shall be drown'd:
        Far be it from me, with too curious Mind,
        To search the Office whence eternal Fate
        Issues her Writs of various Ills to Men;
        Too soon arrested we shall know our Doom,
        And now a present Evil gnaws my Heart.
        Oh! Mother, Mother –
MOTHER PUNCHBOWL: Say, what wou'd my Son?
CAPT. BILKUM: Get me a Wench, and lend me half a Crown.
MOTHER PUNCHBOWL: Thou shalt have both. (I. iii)

15

Such calculated bathos is typical of this light-hearted, amusing little piece.

By this stage of his career, it will be apparent, Fielding had not found any one particular mode which he was content to treat as a repeatable formula for success. He seems to have been experimenting, while prepared to return from time to time to conventional, five-act comedy. Quite why he continued to try writing sentimental comedy, since his undistinguished efforts at it were unpopular, is a mystery. However, despite his excursions into sentimental drama, satire was still very much in evidence in his plays. A short three-act play based on a true story, *The Old Debauchees*, exposes a lecherous Jesuit priest, Father Martin. Martin uses superstition to get his own way, much as Squeezum exploits the law to commit rape, and Richly exploits his own wealth to satisfy his sexual desires. By the customary trickery of disguises, the loathsome Martin is caught by Old and Young Laroon and is turned out to be ducked in a pond and tossed in a blanket then to be disgraced by the priesthood. The vulnerable heroine, Isabel, is clever and quick-witted, but her virtue is hardly stressed at all. The two fathers, Old Laroon and Jourdain, are confirmed sinners, so that Fielding does not present a simple contrast between virtue and vice as he does in some of his earlier plays, and as sentimental dramatists almost always did. Here, the characters who might be victims of the priest's abuse of his privileged position are those we identify or sympathise with, but they are imperfect human beings. Our attention is drawn less to their imperfections than to the contrasting, unsympathetic machinations of Martin. The dominant idea of the play is that the villain is finally exposed by his own villainy – like Squeezum, the priest is caught in his own trap. It is a theme to which Fielding loves to return.

In this same productive year, 1732, Fielding brought out his adaptation of Molière's *Le Médecin malgré lui*, translated as *The Mock Doctor: Or the Dumb Lady Cur'd*. The main interest in this brief, farcical ballad opera comes not so much from the promised satire of physicians as from the ridiculous posturing and drivelling of Gregory, the man who pretends to be a doctor. The tone of the play, like that of Molière's original, is genial and absurd rather than biting. Gregory, for instance, has picked up a tiny smattering of 'physick', as he boasts to his wife: she, wanting revenge for a beating, tells two yokels in search of a doctor for their master Sir Jasper's mysteriously dumb daughter that if they beat Gregory enough, he will admit that he is a physician. As it turns out, he would admit anything to stop them from cudgelling him. He begins to wonder if he really is a doctor and, once he has received his first fee, decides he must be. Gregory revels in his new role, blarneying through all difficulties, prescribing punch instead of medicine, and trotting out some impressive-sounding Latin (once he knows that Sir Jasper will not understand it). Although Fielding exposes the incompetence of doctors, his friendly satire exposes the absurdity of a man's pretending to be what he is not.

In the following year, 1733, Fielding was using Molière again, in *The Miser*, a play translated from *L'Avare*, itself derived from Plautus' *Aulularia*. The extent of Fielding's innovations is small, but significant. Translations are often overlooked in critical discussion, because they are the original work of someone else. But to overlook *The Miser* is to ignore the best translation in English of *L'Avare*, and it is to ignore a crucial debt in Fielding's development as a writer. This Molière comedy is consistent with the aims of Fielding's original comedies and farces of 1732. The central character, Lovegold (Harpagon in *L'Avare*), is predictably willing to sacrifice everything to money. A gross caricature, Lovegold seems to have come from the same stable as Richly and Squeezum. The prologue ('written by a friend') speaks of the decline of modern comedy since the high standards set by Ben Jonson, so that modern characters are seldom drawn 'from Nature' (vii). These allusions make comparison between Lovegold and Volpone inevitable: Lovegold too worships money, but without the pleasure of the chase that Volpone loves so much. The loathsome Lovegold is just as plausible as Volpone, and more realistically paranoid. Lovegold is even prepared to hang himself to avoid losing £10,000!

Lovegold is even more sordid and avaricious than either Volpone or Harpagon. In scenes that follow Molière closely, Lovegold absurdly but monomaniacally repeats the magic words 'Without a Portion' as he gloats at the thought of marrying off his daughter to a man who does not demand a dowry; and later he is the only person in the theatre to be puzzled when his servant James says he can prepare a fine supper if given enough money: 'What, is the Devil in you? always Money. Can you say nothing else, but Money, Money, Money? All my Servants, my Children, my Relations, can pronounce no other Word than Money' (III. iii). But one scene not found in Molière nor in Shadwell's translation of the same play nor in Plautus is III. vii, where Frederick, who loves Mariana, thinks she cannot possibly be serious in accepting old Lovegold's proposal of marriage. She breezily destroys Frederick's confidence with a reminder of a corrupt, degenerate attitude that Fielding cannot leave alone. Although Lovegold is loathsome, we can laugh at him, but we are unlikely to laugh at these words of Mariana's:

Money; Money the most charming of all Things; Money, which will say more in one Moment than the most elegant Lover can in Years. Perhaps you will say a Man is not young; I answer, he is rich. He is not genteel, handsome, witty, brave, good-humour'd; but he is rich, rich, rich, rich, rich – that one Word contradicts every thing you can say against him; and if you were to praise a Person for a whole Hour, and end with, *But he is poor*, you overthrow all you have said; for it has long been an establish'd Maxim, that he who is rich can have no Vice, and he that is poor can have no Virtue. (III. vii)

Mariana does change her mind and marries Frederick, whose sister is also married in a brief sentimental finale. But the play ends on a satirical note, with the other happy bridegroom, Clermont, declaring that 'Avarice, which too often attends Wealth, is a greater Evil than any that is found in Poverty. Misery is generally the End of all Vice; but it is the very Mark at which Avarice seems to aim; the *Miser* endeavours to be wretched' (V. xii).

Fielding followed *The Miser* with another translation, this time from Jean François Regnard's comedy *Le Retour imprévu*, rendered as *The Intriguing Chambermaid* (1734). Fielding reveals in his dedication to Kitty Clive that his drama was not intended to separate examples to be avoided from examples to be imitated: 'But while I hold the Pen, it will be a Maxim with me, that Vice can never be too great to be lashed, nor Virtue too obscure to be commended; in other Words, that Satire can never rise too high, nor Panegyrick stoop too low' (iv). The villains in Fielding's plays are usually set off against the virtuous. In this good-natured comedy there is no real villain, but a wastrel, Valentine, who is 'saved' by the generosity of his father (whose *retour* is *imprévu*), whose name, significantly, is Goodall. He settles his son's debts, thus provoking Lord Puff to splutter to Lord Pride: 'That ever such Plebeian Scoundrels, who are oblig'd to pay their Debts, shou'd presume to engage with us Men of Quality, who are not!' (II. viii). Fielding had learned to control this kind of dichotomy in his plays: the honest, often simple, and virtuous characters contrast in just such neat, balanced formulations with the puffed-up, the proud, the silly, and the really evil characters. Satire describes the latter, sentiment the former group.

Later in 1734 Fielding rewrote *Don Quixote in England*, a ballad opera which he had begun while he was still a student at Leiden in 1728 and to which he now added scenes suggested by the general election of 1734. The dedication to Lord Chesterfield was a public statement that Fielding had joined the opposition; it also confirms that Fielding's purpose was to write satiric comedy:

The Freedom of the Stage is, perhaps, as well worth contending for, as that of the Press. It is the Opinion of an Author well known to Your Lordship, that Examples work quicker and stronger on the Minds of Men than Precepts.

This will, I believe, my Lord, be found truer with regard to Politicks than to Ethicks: the most ridiculous Exhibitions of Luxury or Avarice may likely have little Effect on the Sensualist or the Miser; but I fansy [sic] a lively Representation of the Calamities brought on a Country by general Corruption, might have a very sensible and useful Effect on the Spectators.

Equally important, Fielding stated in his preface that 'Human Nature is every where the same. And the Modes and Habits of particular Nations do not change it enough, sufficiently to distinguish a *Quixote* in *England* from a *Quixote* in *Spain*.'

Primed, therefore, to expect satiric examples which we may apply as we see fit, we are presented with yet another introduction in imitation of *The Beggar's Opera*. And like Gay, Fielding draws attention in a prologue to the absence of a prologue. Fielding must have been confident of his audience by now, for the whole comedy shows his controlled assurance. Amid slapstick farce, with serious elements of political and social satire, Quixote launches into a long and surprisingly defiant statement:

Virtue . . . is too bright for [men's] Eyes, and they dare not behold her. Hypocrisy is the Deity they worship. Is not the Lawyer often call'd an honest Man, when for a sneaking Fee he pleads the Villain's Cause, or attempts to extort Evidence to the Conviction of the Innocent? Does not the Physician live well in his Neighbourhood, while he suffers them to bribe his Ignorance to their Destruction? But why should I mention those whose Profession 'tis to prey on others? Look thro' the World, What is it recommends Men, but the Poverty, the Vice, and the Misery of others? This, *Sancho*, they are sensible of, and therefore, instead of endeavouring to make himself better, each Man endeavours to make his Neighbour worse. Each Man rises to Admiration by trading on Mankind. Riches and Power accrue to the One, by the Destruction of Thousands. These are the general Objects of the good Opinion of Men: Nay, and that which is profess'd to be paid to Virtue, is seldom more to any thing than a supercilious Contempt of our Neighbour. What is a good-natur'd Man? Why, one, who seeing the Want of his Friend, cries he pities him. Is this real? No: If it was, he would relieve him. His Pity is triumphant Arrogance and Insult: It arises from Pride, not from his Compassion. *Sancho*, let them call me mad; I'm not mad enough to court their Approbation. (II.i)

This deeply humane understanding of compassion and contempt, charity and greed, is not really in keeping with the overall tone of the play. In the end Quixote pronounces the grasping doctor and lawyer more mad than himself. True madness, as the final air suggests, does not comprise the Don's imaginary romances and adventures, but a frenzy for material gain at the expense of one's fellow men. This social theme, linked with the play's explicitly political one, expresses the opposition view that political corruption was responsible for moral corruption at all levels of society. It had been easy to score off the traditional greed of the lawyer, the doctor, and the clergyman, but Fielding now transcended this sort of material to create a much more substantial and coherent idea of a society where the apparent madman is profoundly sane and unusually honest. Real madness is a dangerous form of corruption.

Fielding's next play, *An Old Man Taught Wisdom* (1735), did not develop the theme, but instead portrayed three arrant coxcombs trying to win the hand of a rich old man's young daughter. She marries a footman, who knows 'that no one is respected for what he is, but for what he has; the World pays no regard at present to any thing but Money'. This short ballad opera is primarily an entertainment based on the presentation of fools, and only secondarily (yet powerfully) an exploration of the theme that virtue and merit should be more important than money. This had become one of Fielding's favourite themes.

When performed in 1742, this play was followed by *Miss Lucy in Town*, which may have been written in collaboration with David Garrick. *Miss Lucy*, a farce, is reminiscent of *The Country Wife* and *Love for Love* in some respects, but with the added nastiness of a brothel madam trying to capture an innocent country virgin. It reminds one of Hogarth's *Harlot's Progress* and later, Cleland's *Fanny Hill*. Miss Lucy is starry-eyed about London, and nearly meets disaster because she swallows what she is told about 'fashion'. It is ironic that what she hears is true: she does not condemn it, but the audience (presumably) does:

Fine Ladies do every Thing because it's the Fashion. They spoil their Shapes, to appear big with Child, because it's the Fashion. They lose their Money at Whisk [*sic*], without understanding the Game; they go to

Auctions, without intending to buy; they go to Operas, without any Ear; and slight their husbands without disliking them; and all – because it is the Fashion. (8)

And lest we still ask what happens at a masquerade, here is the answer: fine ladies 'dress themselves in a strange Dress, and they walk up and down the Room, and they cry, *Do you know me?* and then they burst out a laughing, and then they sit down, and then they get up, and then they walk about again, and then they go home' (6). Miss Lucy is excited at the prospect of such riveting entertainment. But before she can be ensnared by the corrupt, Miss Lucy is saved by her father, Goodwill, who prefers the country, 'where there is still something of Old *England* remaining' (42–3), and whose principles constitute another of Fielding's rejections of all that the city has come to stand for: 'Henceforth, I will know no Degree, no Difference between Men, but what the Standards of Honour and Virtue create: The noblest Birth without these is but splendid Infamy; and a Footman with these Qualities, is a Man of Honour' (43). Fielding was increasingly concerned to expose the artificiality of rank and to celebrate the innate qualities of virtue and honour.

In 1735 Fielding wrote one of the world's dullest plays, *The Universal Gallant*. Contemporary audiences thought that this non-satiric comedy was appalling, and attacked it with a violence that Fielding felt obliged to counter. His preface exposes him as a man seared by criticism that he considered unfair, 'cruel', and prejudiced. His reaction was uncharacteristically bitter, but then the play is uncharacteristically awful.

By contrast, three of Fielding's last plays – *Pasquin* (1736), *Tumble-Down Dick* (1736), and *The Historical Register for the Year 1736* (1737) – were great popular successes. All three use the 'rehearsal' formula, in which the supposed author directs the players and discusses his play with a critic or some other commentator. As they sit watching a farce being played, the characters in the frame action are satiric commentators who interpret the play-within-the-play, often showing us how to understand what we see. The audience cannot mistake Fielding's satiric intentions.

In *Pasquin*, Trapwit declares that he has written his comedy 'in the exact and true Spirit of *Molière*; and this I will say for it, that except about a Dozen, or a Score, or so, there is not one impure Joke in it' (5). Trapwit's comedy-within-the-play concerns an election campaign, where bribery is so prominent and topical an issue that the tragic poet, Fustian, asks, 'Is there nothing but Bribery in this

Play of yours, Mr. *Trapwit?*'(8). In the Jonsonian tradition that Fielding had adapted for his own purposes, Trapwit replies, 'Sir, this Play is an exact Representation of Nature' (8). The frame action of *Pasquin* satirises modern comedy, while Trapwit's comedy itself satirises both the dishonesty and the rhetoric of modern politics.

The second half of *Pasquin* is perhaps less accessible to the modern reader than the first, since it contains a tragedy-within-the-play, again sending up bombastic contemporary tragedy. The hallmarks of Fielding's satiric comedy are here, too, in Fustian's tragedy. His unfortunate heroine, Queen Common Sense, opens the tragedy by bitching at the unfairness of the law; and, in due course, priests and physicians take their customary positions alongside lawyers as corrupt parasites. Wondering if Fustian's 'Satire on Law and Physick' might be 'somewhat too general', Sneerwell the critic receives the satirist's standard reply: 'What is said here cannot hurt either an honest Lawyer, or a good Physician; and such may be, nay, I know such are: If the Opposites to these are the most general, I cannot help that' (46–7). The whole of Fustian's tragedy is a pretext to satirise the theatre and vitiated public taste, for both are dominated by Queen Ignorance: the result is that little serious drama is presented on the London stage, but an excess of pantomime, rope-dancing, puppet shows, and other 'low' entertainments. Fustian's play is in fact remarkably close to those he sets out to satirise.

Although the political jokes and allusions in *Pasquin* may seem to be even-handedly distributed between the two main parties, the final stance of Fielding's lamenting a decline in taste ranges him with the opposition satirists. Pope, by 1736 an acknowledged 'opposition' poet, had exploited the connection between the corruption of the theatre managements and corruption in government. Fielding himself had already used the theatrical metaphor to satirise politicians, as had the *Craftsman* and *Fog's Weekly Journal*. In such formulations, 'corruption' never applies to the opposition, nor to politicians in general, but to Walpole and his immediate supporters. *Pasquin*'s political satire is somewhat generalised, as it is in *Tumble-Down Dick*, whose burden is to attack the unfairness of a corrupt society in which the rich escape, but the poor do not. Following on from Fustian, *Tumble-Down Dick* is an example of the 'low' entertainment that it satirises.

In 1737 Fielding made a mistake with a less ingenious play, *Eurydice*, which relates the classical myth of Orpheus and Eurydice as a farce that contains mild social and political satire. The play's abject but undeserved failure stung its author. Rather than repeat the sniping disillusionment of his preface to *The Universal Gallant*, Fielding retorted with *Eurydice Hiss'd*, a clever, witty satire on 'the town'.

Fielding reserved the greatest success of his entire theatrical career until 1737, when *The Historical Register* was produced at the New Theatre in the Haymarket. This play is a hilarious farce, which pleased its audiences as much as it irritated the first minister. In the preface Fielding once again indicated that his political sympathy lay entirely with the opposition, as he launched a broadside attack on corruption. Fielding's attack is obviously meant to hit Walpole, but there would be some justice in the claim that his prime target is the vice:

I shall only observe, that Corruption hath the same Influence on all Societies, all Bodies, where we see it always produce an entire Destruction and total Change: For which Reason, whoever attempteth to introduce Corruption into any Community, doth much the same Thing, and ought to be treated in much the same Manner, with him who poisoneth a Fountain, in order to disperse a Contagion, which he is sure every one will drink of.

(vii)

Many local and topical allusions, and the satiric commentary of the frame action, support this general theme of exposing corruption. The 'fount of corruption' as Walpole was sometimes called in the press, is implicitly responsible for corruption in virtually every aspect of British life. The central scene involves an auction in which nearly all the lots awaken little or no demand and are left unsold. The lots include a political cloak 'only proper for the Country', a piece of patriotism, three grains of modesty, 'A very neat clear Conscience, which has been worn by a Judge and a Bishop', the cardinal virtues (introduced by mistake for a cardinal's virtues), a great deal of wit, and one lot for which the brisk bidding soon reaches £1,000: 'a very considerable Quantity of Interest at Court'.

Although, again, Fielding seems to be equally inclined to satirise the ministry and the opposition, as Medley the author claims, his satire is directed at Walpole. Sharing the view expressed by the opposition satirists, Fielding held Walpole ultimately responsible for the decline of modern drama, since such decline was symptomatic of a more widespread corruption. Medley avers

a strict Resemblance between the States Political and Theatrical; there is a

Ministry in the latter as well as the former, and I believe as weak a Ministry
as any poor Kingdom cou'd ever boast of; Parts are given in the latter to
Actors, with much the same Regard to Capacity, as Places in the former
have some Times been, in former Ages I mean; and tho' the Publick damn
both, yet while they both receive their Pay, they laugh at the Publick behind
the Scenes; and if one considers the Plays that come from one Part, and the
Writings from the other, one would be apt to think the same Author's were
retain'd in both . . .   (18)

Medley's statement refers to his portrayal of Pistol's (that is,
Theophilus Cibber's) 'ministerial' capacity when he 'thinks himself
a great man'. Pistol then calls himself a 'Prime Minister Theatrical'
(II. i). There is no room for oblique innuendo where the satire is this
explicit.

In the middle of 1737 Fielding's dramatic career was rudely cut
short by the Licensing Act. The traditional view is that the measure
was designed primarily to silence Fielding himself, who had now
become second only to Cibber in popularity. Fielding could have
gone on as a professional dramatist if he had wanted to, but only by
excising political commitment from his plays. Since his main
concern by the mid-1730s was with political satire, his decision to
quit the theatre was virtually forced on him. Although in writing
political satire Fielding did not abandon the sentimental, but
blended sentiment and satire to show examples of virtue and vice,
his dramatic satires offer less of the sentimental, fewer examples of
virtue, and many more of vice. In these late plays he owes less to
Cibber and Steele than to Gay and Molière, and to Buckingham for
the 'rehearsal' format.

Like Molière, who does not celebrate – nor even countenance –
the perfectibility of human nature, Fielding, in most of his plays, lets
his vicious characters remain vicious, rather than have them
implausibly reform, while virtue-in-distress comes through its
trials. Like Tartuffe, Harpagon, and Don Juan, the memorable
characters from Fielding's drama are the least attractive ones:
Squeezum, Richly, Martin. In the dramatic satires, few characters
are memorable at all, since character is less important than fast
action and absurd situations, deflation of pretension, satirical
exposures of the state of the theatre, politics, and morality. Fully
rounded characters are unnecessary to achieve these aims:
suggestive caricatures will do. In all Fielding's comedies, his
characters tend towards types, or humours. His presentation of
characters depends on an irony shared between himself and his
audience, as is usual in satiric comedy. In the earlier plays, that

irony is frequently supplied by Fielding's prologues and prefaces, which are not of course part of the audience's experience in the theatre. In the dramatic satires, the irony is supplied by an outside observer in the frame action.

Of the numerous thematic and aesthetic affinities that have been noticed between Fielding's plays and his novels, the most striking are: his characterisation; his satire of corruption, meanness, and hypocrisy; his tendency to ridicule by burlesque exaggeration and parodic incongruity; and his use of a satiric commentator. However, Fielding did not turn directly from drama to the novel. Almost as soon as he was obliged to leave the theatre, he took to the law. When he emerged again as a public writer, a satirist barred from the stage, he became a journalist.

On 15 November 1739 the first issue of the *Champion: or British Mercury* was published. This paper, which came out on Tuesdays, Thursdays, and Saturdays, contained a leading article as well as news, commentary, advertisements (of which a few were satirical), and sometimes a 'literary article'. The leading articles and a selection of the other material from the first ninety-four numbers (that is, up to 19 June 1740) were reprinted in two volumes in 1741. Although the *Champion* continued well into 1742, no more papers were reprinted. Copies of the original papers are even more scarce than most eighteenth-century newspapers, and determining who wrote many of them is also difficult. Fielding's partner in the enterprise was James Ralph, a competent and outspoken essayist from Philadelphia who got nowhere by supporting Walpole and so turned against him. Although contributions were sent in by other people – some probably unidentified even by the editors – Fielding and Ralph wrote most of the papers. In the 1741 edition Fielding's preface attributed, by means of code letters, sixty-three essays to himself, eighteen to Ralph. Twenty essays were not attributed to anyone. The reprinted political news was usually, but not always, Ralph's. Fielding continued to contribute to the *Champion* until some time in 1741, but it is uncertain which essays he wrote after the first ninety-four issues. I shall restrict myself here to those essays included in the 1741 edition.

The *Champion* seems to have been only moderately popular. An early issue (no. 9; 4 December 1739) contained three letters on the *Champion*'s quality, one ironically accusing it of being dull and asking the editor to 'infuse Gall into your Ink, and, instead of Morality, Wit, and Humour, deal forth private Slander and

Abuse'. The other two letters tell of the *Champion*'s favourable reception at London coffee houses, but in no. 15 (18 December 1739) even Fielding himself admits that the *Champion* is not doing very well yet. With no. 64 (10 April 1740) it became an evening paper, with a modified title, the *Champion: or Evening Advertiser*, presumably in a bid to increase sales. On the whole, the paper was probably less successful than the two principal opposition newspapers, *Common Sense* and the *Craftsman*, whose ally the *Champion* was consciously intended to be. Those two sold about 2,000 each.

The general political stance of the *Champion*, together with several complimentary allusions to these other newspapers, aligned it firmly with the opposition press. However, the tone and range of its essays were obviously meant to imitate the *Spectator*. Rather than innovating, the editors of the *Champion* were content to emulate the established formulae of successful journals. This policy could have resulted in a stale rehashing of old material, but it did not: the *Champion* is lively, entertaining, and varied.

It is generally accepted that Fielding's experience on the *Champion* played an important part in his development as a novelist. As a journalist, Fielding learned to exploit the wide variety of satiric forms developed in the press since the beginning of the century. He also learned to write the discursive address, directed to a much more diffuse and anonymous audience than he would find in the theatre. In particular, the form of the essay periodical provided him with the chance to create a fictional editor, like Mr Spectator or Isaac Bickerstaff in the *Tatler* or even Caleb D'Anvers of the *Craftsman*. Fielding seems to have been the inventor of the *Champion*'s persona, Captain Hercules Vinegar – a name combining strength and acerbic wit.[1] Fielding chose not to explore the idea of a persona very far, preferring to stay within the confines established by convention.

In the early numbers Hercules Vinegar introduces the members of his family, each of whom is an expert in some field of activity, but in subsequent issues none of them are as much in evidence as he is himself. Captain Vinegar soon established himself as the champion of good sense, the friend of humility and virtue, the enemy of foppery and dishonesty. In no. 11 (8 December 1739) he introduces an account of his cudgel, which has 'a very strange and almost incredible Quality belonging to it, of falling, of its own Accord, on every egregious Knave who comes in its Way'. In the manner of his polite predecessors, Captain Vinegar thus becomes a satiric

---

[1] Hercules Vinegar was also the name of a contemporary prize-fighter.

guardian of common sense: the victims of his cudgel are '100 Lawyers, 99 Courtiers, 73 Priests, 8 Physicians, and 13 Beaus (whereof 12 died of the first Blow) besides innumerable others'. This role is further developed when Hercules Vinegar instigates a Court of Judicature to try cases that fall outside the law, such as folly, vanity, or abuse of the English language.

Hercules Vinegar is the focus of the paper. Letters are addressed to him and receive his commentary; essays are offered as the products of his pen. This character's function is similar to that of the commentators in the frame action of a 'rehearsal' play. Those commentators react to other people, who are presented dramatically; the narrators thus mediate between dramatic characters and the audience, or reader. Most readers of the *Champion* now recognise in Hercules Vinegar the prototype of the narrator who conducts us through *Joseph Andrews* or *Tom Jones*. The fictional editor of the *Champion* is primarily a vehicle for satire, as the majority of such figures are in early eighteenth-century periodicals.

Fielding's contributions to the paper include many essays on subjects that are treated satirically. For example: the corruption of language (nos. 26–8, 80, 91); the art of lying – which puts him in the company of Arbuthnot and Swift (33); law, divinity, and medicine (18, 40, 53, 59); roguery and folly (51, 53); Colley Cibber (60, 66, 69, 72, 74, 75, 80); vanity (66, 74); and justice (24). Without inventing new satiric forms, Fielding exploited old ones: the dream, or vision (13, 19–20, 63, 71, 78, 83); the parallel between theatre and government (69, 74); the Lucianic dialogue (83); and the ironic commentary. Other essays treated subjects that one associates mainly with the moralist: the imperfections of men (3, 12, 14, 22, 66); virtue (4, 22, 30–2, 48, 49, 74); good nature (58); and charity (41–3, 61), all of which recur in his novels.

Ronald Paulson has suggested that Fielding gradually changed from being a satirist, who only opposed things, to being a moralist, who posited alternatives (*Satire and the Novel*, p. 99). Obviously, this attractive proposition requires that 'satire' means not positing alternatives. Satire in Fielding's hands clearly has an essential moral function, even if its main purpose is destructive. To Fielding, as to many of his contemporaries, 'satire' meant the opposite of 'panegyric' and, as he said in *The Intriguing Chambermaid*, he offered examples to be emulated as well as examples to be avoided. Together, these disparate examples express dissatisfaction (what he would call satire) and alternatives (what he would call panegyric). Certainly, some of the *Champion* essays combine both kinds of example, as the plays do, but frequently with less emphasis than before on the vicious and more on the virtuous.

In the six years between the Licensing Act and 1743, Fielding published his essays in the *Champion*, a translation of Gustavus Adlerfeld's *Military History of Charles XII, King of Sweden*, a poem, four pamphlets, a new play (though from old materials), a collaborative translation of Aristophanes' comedy, *Plutus*, plus probably his own best-known satire, *Jonathan Wild* (as part of a three-volume set of miscellaneous writings), and his first novel, *Joseph Andrews*. These were financially desperate years, but they were fruitful.

2

The *Miscellanies* and *Jonathan Wild*

At some time in 1741, presumably after he left the *Champion*, Fielding probably began to collect and revise his miscellaneous poems and essays for publication in the winter of 1741-2. On 5 June 1742 the *Daily Post* advertised a prospectus (the earliest to have survived) for three volumes of Fielding's *Miscellanies* to be published by subscription at one guinea a set or two guineas for the 'Royal Paper' edition. This method of publication required subscribers to pay one half of the price in advance as a deposit, the other half when they received the books. In return their names were listed at the front of volume one. Fielding therefore received a desperately needed cash advance.

Most of the subscribers on Fielding's impressive list came from the theatre, the law, and politics. As expected, the opposition was well represented, but Walpole (who took ten sets) and his sympathisers were there too. Having put up with several long delays, the patient subscribers finally got the *Miscellanies* on 7 April 1743. Although the *Miscellanies* postdate *Joseph Andrews* by more than a year, most of the materials had been conceived and drafted, though not necessarily finished, earlier.

The first volume of the *Miscellanies* contains five serious poems, thirty-three light verses, three formal prose essays, and six dramatic and minor prose pieces. According to the 1742 prospectus the whole of volume two was to have been given over to *A Journey from this World to the Next*, but, presumably because this piece was unfinished, the volume finally had to be filled out with two plays: *Eurydice* (staged in 1737) and *The Wedding Day*, hastily prepared from old material for a production by Fielding's friend David Garrick in February 1743. The third volume was entirely occupied by *Jonathan Wild*. There is an improvised air about the whole collection, not only because of its intentionally miscellaneous character, but because of the impression it conveys that Fielding was writing under great pressure, unable to finish some pieces, and filling spaces with anything that came to hand until the last moment. Even the two longest and most significant pieces, the unfinished *Journey* and *Jonathan Wild*, are demonstrably patchwork in places.

29

Most of the light verse in volume one is insignificant, much of it consisting of conventional amorous trifles. Although the five serious verse essays, all conscious imitations of Pope, are poor poems, they show Fielding confronting five important subjects: greatness, good nature, liberty, marriage, and human inconsistency. All five are worked into the ethical basis of *Jonathan Wild*. While the light prose is all satirical, the two most serious prose pieces in volume one – *An Essay on Conversation* and *An Essay on the Knowledge of the Characters of Men* – are moral treatises rather than satirical exposures of vice. Nevertheless, Fielding said that in the latter he had 'endeavoured to expose . . . Hypocrisy; the Bane of all Virtue, Morality, and Goodness; and to arm, as well as I can, the honest, undesigning, open-hearted Man, who is generally the Prey of this Monster, against it' (*Miscellanies*, I, preface, p. 4). This sounds, in fact, like a statement of satirical intent.

The main work in volume two, *A Journey from this World to the Next*, is underrated. Although, because it is unfinished, the text plainly cannot satisfy a reader who demands the symmetries of neoclassical form, it provides ample compensations. Like several shorter pieces elsewhere in the *Miscellanies* and in the *Champion*, Fielding's narrative is derived from Lucian, the second-century Greek satirist. The *Journey* is based on elements of four Lucianic satires, which characteristically present naive travellers who, in another land or another world, put questions to the spirits of famous dead men. The inhabitants of the other world are customarily objective, honest, and clearsighted, in contrast to their visitors, the faults of whose own world are ruthlessly exposed. One of Lucian's favourite forms, the fantasy voyage to another world was a useful vehicle for satire. This form allows the author to distinguish truth from lies, and actions from words. In a more recent precedent, Swift had Gulliver encounter famous dead authors in Glubbdubdrib (*Gulliver's Travels*, book 3). Like Lucian and Swift, Fielding attacks corruption, the frauds of the learned professions, and hypocrisy, against which he wages war because 'most Mischiefs (especially those which fall on the worthiest Part of Mankind) owe their Original to this detestable Vice' (*Miscellanies*, I, preface, p. 4). But Fielding's attack is less severe than Swift's, less cynical than Lucian's.

The first nine chapters of the *Journey* tell the story of a narrator recently deceased, who is transported through the next world to the gate of Elysium. At the gate, the spirits of dead people present themselves to Minos, who judges their behaviour on earth and accordingly admits them to Elysium, consigns them to the bottomless pit, or sends them back to earth to try again. To all spirits preparing to return to earth, Fortune offers lots 'as equal as possible to each other' (I, 6). Hence it is the fortune of a poet to endure contempt but to enjoy self-satisfaction; a philosopher, poverty but ease; a prime minister, disgrace (nothing else); and a patriot, glory: 'indeed the whole seemed to contain such a mixture of good and evil, that it would have puzzled me which to chuse' (I, 6). This is plainly a formulaic way of satirising character types.

Himself allowed to enter Elysium, the narrator begins to describe some of the people he meets there. These include Richard Glover, nowadays a forgotten poet; Orpheus and Sappho; Homer, with the critic 'Madam Dacier sat in his lap'; Virgil, Addison, and Steele; Shakespeare and two actors, Betterton and Booth; Tom Thumb; Oliver Cromwell and Charles I; Livy; and finally, Julian the Apostate. The historical Julian marked his brief reign as Roman Emperor in the fourth century by declaring himself a pagan and granting general religious toleration. As Lucian had introduced *Of True History* by admitting that it is all lies, so Fielding admits that his treatment of Julian has 'done many Violences to History, and mixed Truth and Falshood with much Freedom . . . I profess Fiction only' (*Miscellanies*, I, preface, p. 4). Anyway, Fielding is not concerned with the famous aspects of Julian's life. Instead, the imaginary adventures of Julian in successive incarnations occupy chapters 10 to 25. The narrative then breaks off abruptly leaving Julian's story unresolved, because 'part of the manuscript is lost', and it moves directly to 'Book XIX, chapter 7, Wherein Anna Boleyn relates the history of her life'. At the end of this fragment, a note explains:

Here ends this curious manuscript; the rest being destroyed in rolling up pens, tobacco, &c. It is to be hoped heedless people will henceforth be more cautious what they burn, or use to other vile purposes; especially when they consider the fate which had likely to have befallen the divine Milton, and that the works of Homer were probably discovered in some chandler's shop in Greece.

Since Fielding did not finish the *Journey*, he adopted an old trick by pretending that the narrative was a fragmentary manuscript. That is the fiction used to explain why the *Journey* has a beginning and a middle but no end.

Back in 1731 Fielding had pretended that the *Tragedy of Tragedies* was a new-found manuscript. As then, so now in the *Journey*, Fielding's intentions are satirical, since he is again imitating Swift and Pope. Unlike the Scriblerians, however, Fielding does not follow the device through with an elaborate apparatus of mock-scholarly footnotes, yet his few notes to the *Journey* are significant. Where Swift uses such notes in a forthright way to attack specific opponents, Fielding mocks only the idea of the literal-minded annotator who prepares learned commentary on trifles. In the *Journey* the annotator is the narrator, who becomes a character with superior knowledge, at times condescending to his readers and twice telling them how they must interpret the satiric points.

One footnote tells us that 'in the panegyrical part of this work some particular person is always meant: but, in the satirical, nobody' (I, 3). A more jocose note in the preceding chapter invites 'every lady of quality, or no quality . . . to apply the character to themselves' (I, 2). The 'character' there is one whose 'countenance displayed all the cheerfulness, the good-nature, and the modesty, which diffuse such brightness round the beauty of Seraphina, awing every beholder with respect, and, at the same time, ravishing him with admiration' (I, 2). Seraphina may be the object of panegyric, but the ladies of quality – or no quality – must be the objects of satire. This mild, good-natured satire incongruously contrasts the implied reality with the satiric victims' flattering image of themselves. In the text itself, the same incongruity exposes the vanity of fashionable gentlemen who carry amber-headed canes and affect to be more genteel than they are. Such knowable creatures from this world are, in the next, mere street-porters, whose canes have become the insignia, or 'tickets', of humble office. Similarly, in Elysium arrogant commentators quibble over trifles that cause the authors not even momentary concern. In chapter 4 Fielding genially satirises 'the formality of a court, notwithstanding its outward splendour and magnificence'. It is less important that this court is situated in 'the palace of Death' than that the place offers a disparity between the vast, sumptuous palace and the boring, trivial formalities, between outward appearance and inward truth. All these incongruous discrepancies explicitly contrast true and false values.

In the other world, the masks of hypocrisy are torn off. We obviously take the exposure as a satiric exposure of human motives in this world, because the fiction is controlled by a reliable if rather distant narrator who stands on the side of virtue and truth. The ninth chapter ends with the narrator admitted to Elysium, having proved himself sufficiently virtuous. By this stage he has also established himself as a knowledgeable, genial, and vivid character – by no means the dupe that Gulliver turns out to be. But once the narrator tells us in chapter 10 of his meeting with Julian, he virtually disappears for the rest of the book. His place is taken by Julian, apparently a rather unlikely candidate for a sympathetic narrative role. However, Julian brings to the narrative an almost confessional openness, which can convey regret for indulging a past vice, or some similarly 'honest' reaction to his own sins and crimes: these are admissions never (so it is implied) made on earth.

Fielding's apology about his historical accuracy in presenting Julian's history seems superfluous, since Julian has an authorial presence but no historical identity. The narrator of chapters 10 to 25 could be anyone: only the chapter headings remind us that his name is Julian. The connecting feature of this part of the narrative is that each chapter describes another transmigration. Each one resembles the kind of self-contained essay that could have been a suitable contribution to the *Champion* (indeed one of them was). The sixteen chapters thus contain a broad, representative, loosely connected series of satiric character sketches, as the introduction to this sequence promises,

he had been denied admittance [to Elysium], and forced to undergo several subsequent pilgrimages on earth, and to act in the different characters of a slave, a Jew, a general, an heir, a carpenter, a beau, a monk, a fiddler, a wise man, a king, a fool, a beggar, a prince, a statesman, a soldier, a taylor, an alderman, a poet, a knight, a dancing-master, and three times a bishop, before his martyrdom, which, together with his behaviour in this last character, satisfied the judge, and procured him a passage to the blessed regions.   (I, 10)

The satire is directed not only at these characters that Julian adopts, but also at those he encounters. Hence, Julian recalls an episode that does credit neither to himself in the character of a king, because he formed 'a very unjust opinion' of his 'whole people', nor to his ministers, because they planted such opinions in his mind. He reflects:

This is a trick, I believe, too often played with sovereigns, who, by such means, are prevented from that open intercourse with their subjects which, as it would greatly endear the person of the prince to the people, so might it often prove dangerous to a minister who was consulting his own interest only at the expense of both.   (I, 17)

Incidentally, this chimes nicely with opposition allegations that by

refusing to allow the British people access to George II, Walpole
protected himself. In other chapters, Julian recounts some of the
dirty tricks he himself learned, but usually there is a rough charm in
his tales of behaviour that is never good enough to get him into
Elysium, nor reprobate enough to warrant his descent into the
bottomless pit. All in all Julian is a mixture of good and evil, as is
each milieu in which he has found himself.

The extraneous chapter about Anne Boleyn, which follows
Julian's narrative, is attributed in a footnote to 'a woman's hand'
and has therefore been thought to be the work of the novelist Sarah
Fielding, Henry's sister. Whoever wrote it, the chapter is feeble and
tedious, and to judge by its nineteen-page-long paragraph, it is
probably an unrevised makeweight.

The genial satire of the *Journey* posits a different world where
actions match words and where, therefore, human motivations are
not concealed. By contrast, in this world of ours full of vanity and
hypocrisy, actions do not match words and deceit can hurt the
innocent. Like Hercules Vinegar at his Court of Judicature, Minos
at the gate of Elysium can expose people for what they are because
he can see through their pretences: in a less direct way, so can the
narrator of the *Journey*. Parts of the *Journey* thus anticipate the
extended irony of *Jonathan Wild*, a satire in which the relationship
between word and deed is crucial.

In *Jonathan Wild* the concepts of 'goodness' and 'greatness'
dominate the narrative, to the extent of being the goals of those who
either do or do not match their words with appropriate actions. In a
characteristically allegorical passage the *Journey* prepares the
ground for these concepts too, since

we discovered two large roads leading different ways, and of very different
appearance; the one all craggy with rocks, full as it seemed of boggy
grounds, and everywhere beset with briars, so that it was impossible to pass
through it without the utmost danger and difficulty; the other, the most
delightful imaginable, leading through the most verdant meadows, painted
and perfumed with all kinds of beautiful flowers; in short, the most wanton
imagination could imagine nothing more lovely. Notwithstanding which,
we were surprized to see great numbers crowding into the former, and only
one or two solitary spirits chusing the latter. On enquiry, we were
acquainted that the bad road was the way to greatness, and the other to
goodness.   (I, 5)

So, although 'the greatest and truest happiness which this world
affords, is to be found only in the possession of goodness and virtue'

THE *MISCELLANIES* AND *JONATHAN WILD*

(Introduction), the 'minds of men' are unwilling to relinquish the idea that greatness is more desirable. This is Fielding's variation on a traditional theme.

Fielding created in *Jonathan Wild* an ostensible panegyric of a vicious criminal, Wild, whom he relentlessly dubs 'great'. He also created an ostensible satire of an ordinary but virtuous jeweller, Thomas Heartfree, whom he relentlessly dubs 'good'. With the help of a gang of ruffians, Wild tries to ruin Heartfree and rape his wife. Glorious Vice thus fiercely persecutes contemptible Virtue: but Vice is finally punished and Virtue elevated to dizzy heights, as Wild goes to the gallows and Heartfree prospers beyond his wildest dreams.

The real Jonathan Wild was a notorious criminal, who styled himself 'Thief-Taker General of Great Britain and Ireland'. This title implies that Wild was on the side of the law against the criminal. But he made himself head of a gang, whose precarious unity he preserved by bribery and the law of violence. At his instigation the gang stole goods, which Wild then restored to the owners, who paid him a reward for doing so. Wild was finally executed at Tyburn on 24 May 1725, having received probably more publicity than any other criminal of the age. He was the subject of numerous 'biographies', ballads, essays, newspaper articles, quasi-religious tracts, and satirical pamphlets, many of which likened this manipulator to Walpole. Many of the 'biographers' of Wild and other criminals pictured their subjects as romantic adventurers, thus glamorising crime and the criminal. After portraying lives full of ingenuity, successful sexual exploits, and dangerous hazards negotiated, some biographies came to a perfunctory moralising end with the implausibly repentant criminals making their way, head bowed, to the next world (that is, Tyburn). Others, of course, had their criminals swaggering to the last. Wild was portrayed both ways.

Fielding's *Jonathan Wild* is in part a response to these criminal biographies. Nobody is quite sure where to place or how to classify *Wild*. Critics cannot even agree that it is a novel, perhaps because its characters and their conflicts are so crude. Biographies, novels, and a host of more minor genres were given the status – in their titles, anyway – of history. Biography of 'great and eminent men', as Fielding has it, is 'properly styled the quintessence of history'. Apart from sounding like a concise guide to the objectives of neoclassical literature, the first paragraph of *Wild* explains that such history should ensure that readers are not only agreeably entertained, but most usefully instructed; for, besides the attaining hence a consummate knowledge of human nature in general; of its secret springs, various windings, and perplexed mazes; we have here before our eyes lively examples of whatever is amiable or detestable, worthy of admiration or abhorrence, and are consequently taught, in a manner infinitely more effectual than by precept, what we are eagerly to imitate or carefully to avoid.   (I, 1)

This paragraph reveals that Fielding's 'panegyric' and 'satire' are combined in his own 'history', in the same relation as they are in his drama. The resulting narrative is exemplary history, in which individual examples of various modes of conduct together create one universal example. By emphasising the general, the first paragraph of *Wild* should warn us that there is no consistent identification of an ideal or a grotesque with any real person.

Fielding does not follow closely any of the previous Wild narratives. He adopts conventions of picaresque fiction by making his protagonist a rogue (a *pícaro*) and by organising the narrative roughly around the chronology of the rogue's life. Even this latter convention is parodied in a chapter that covers eight years of Wild's life in two pages: 'When we consider the ridiculous figure this chapter must make, being the history of no less than eight years, our only comfort is, that the histories of some men's lives, and perhaps of some men who have made a noise in the world, are in reality as absolute blanks as the travels of our hero' (I, 7). Above all, Fielding parodies some formal features of contemporary serious biographies (for instance, the birth and ancestry of the hero; I, 3) and some of the rogue biographies (for instance, the criminal's perfunctory repentance in Newgate, where the chaplain, or 'ordinary', visits him; IV, 13). *Wild* is an inversion of the criminal biography: Fielding ridicules the rogue instead of glorifying him. He was by no means the first writer to treat Jonathan Wild this way.

The History of the Life of Mr. Jonathan Wild the Great has attracted more notice than anything else in the *Miscellanies*. One reason for this interest is that Wild seems to be a satirical analogue of Walpole. But when the *Miscellanies* were eventually published, Walpole had been out of office for over a year and, still notorious or not, Wild had been dead for eighteen years. If the satiric target was Walpole, Fielding was flogging a dead horse. He certainly alludes to Walpole by constantly emphasising the 'great man', who is always willing to break his promises, to operate by bribery, to sacrifice liberty, honour, virtue, and innocence to his own interest; the 'great man' usually escapes the execution he deserves. Since 1726, every one of these characteristics had been used repeatedly in the opposition press campaign against 'a certain Great Man'.

It might have been a belated act of contrition that in a second edition of *Wild* in 1754, Fielding toned down some passages attacking a prime minister. Yet the revised text, which we generally read today, still obviously satirises an unnamed prime minister. By 1754 Walpole had been dead, if not forgotten, for nine years, but his memory was overshadowed by a new generation of politicians. No one can be sure when *Wild* was written or how much of it was changed in manuscript. Much of it was probably composed while Walpole was still securely in power, but this is no reason to suppose that it is or ever was intended to be a satire of Walpole himself. It is consistent with the nature of the political satire of *Wild* that Fielding should add this hint to his preface:

I have been so far from endeavouring to particularize any Individual, that I have with my utmost Art avoided it; so will any such Application be unfair in my reader, especially if he knows much of the Great World, since he must then be acquainted, I believe, with more than one on whom he can fix the Resemblance.   (*Miscellanies*, I, preface, p. 9)

And a late addition to the text develops this hint by condemning the opposition leaders who had removed Walpole in February 1742, but who then fulfilled none of their promises, changed nothing, and merely continued where Walpole had left off (IV, 3). Even if Fielding's disclaimer is ironic, as such disclaimers often are, it still tells us – like the first paragraph of *Wild* itself – that Fielding's satire is general, but we may apply it as we see fit.

Jonathan Wild goes beyond purely topical political satire, not only to achieve a general political aim, but also to expose human weakness, folly, and vice. Because the satire is not exclusively political, one critic has even denied *Wild* any political intent at all. This judgment is ludicrous in view of the allusions to a prime minister and the emphasis on greatness.

The narrative begins and ends with allusions to Alexander the Great and Julius Caesar, both 'great men', whose rapaciousness was a favourite theme among historians and satirists alike. These two criminal emperors are (says Fielding) 'impertinently' praised for a benevolence they did not have: such praise tends to conceal the appalling enormity of their acts of destruction. That they are mentioned at all as examples of greatness indicates Fielding's concern with tyranny and evil in a political context.

It is in this political context that Fielding discusses greatness and goodness. In the preface to the *Miscellanies* he reiterates the 'moral' of the *Beggar's Opera*: 'Nor do I know any thing which can raise an honest Man's Indignation higher than that the same Morals should be in one Place attended with all imaginable Misery and Infamy, and in the other, with the highest Luxury and Honour' (10). But the more interesting part of this prefatory statement is Fielding's justification for having represented greatness 'in so disgraceful and contemptuous a Light' (11). He continues:

The Truth, I apprehend, is, we often confound the Ideas of Goodness and Greatness together, or rather include the former in our Idea of the latter. If this be so, it is surely a great Error, and no less than a Mistake of the Capacity for the Will. In Reality, no Qualities can be more distinct: for as it cannot be doubted but that Benevolence, Honour, Honesty, and Charity, make a good Man; and that Parts, Courage, are the efficient Qualities of a Great Man, so must it be confess'd, that the Ingredients which compose the former of these Characters, bear no Analogy to, nor Dependence on those which constitute the latter. A Man may therefore be Great without being Good, or Good without being Great. (11–12)

It is also possible for a man to be good and great ('the *true Sublime* in Human Nature', (12)), but no such man is the subject of *Wild*. Fielding's purpose is not explicitly to celebrate goodness, but to expose a false conception of 'Bombast Greatness', which arrogates 'not only Riches and Power, but often Honour, or at least the Shadow of it' (13). Fielding's stated purpose therefore is to present a satirical example of vice to be avoided.

Exemplary satire is the basis of *Jonathan Wild*: with some justice, Fielding announces that his 'Narrative is rather of such Actions which [Wild] might have performed, or would, or should have performed, than what he really did; and may, in Reality, as well suit any other such great Man, as the Person himself whose Name it bears . . . Roguery, and not a Rogue, is my Subject' (9). Promising a one-sided allegory, this statement prepares for a satire of evil, but not for a panegyric of virtue. The narrative lives up to the promise, for Wild occupies the centre of the stage, while the few good characters – the Heartfrees and Tom Friendly – are minor and feeble, even for allegorical representations of guileless goodness. The good characters are hopelessly outnumbered by a self-interested, hostile, and corrupt majority, which preys on them. But the good characters are also exemplary, for without victims there would be no villains.

Critics find themselves having to apologise for Heartfree and his somewhat colourless, boring family, because their virtue is so ineffectual ('passive' is the usual label) in contrast to the dynamism of evil. Without a spark of evil in them, the Heartfrees are constantly at the mercy of evil men: indeed, Heartfree 'seems sent into this world as a proper object on which the talents of [Wild] were to be displayed with a proper and just success' (II, 1). The Heartfrees are not totally passive: although they never make anything happen, they are tougher than they look when it comes to resisting their enemies. But they are passive in one crucial sense. Adhering to their Christian virtue, they do not rely on their own actions, but trust that Providence will save them. In fact, Mrs Heartfree's adventures at sea, which she describes at length in an apparent digression, seem to be included only to illustrate what she believes 'is the surest truth, THAT PROVIDENCE WILL SOONER OR LATER PROCURE THE FELICITY OF THE VIRTUOUS AND INNOCENT' (IV, 11). Yet her sequence of hairsbreadth escapes – which she does little to achieve – from a succession of rapists strikes me as darkly funny. Although the Heartfrees are exemplary, they are ineffective precisely because the agency that protects them against the ravages of self-interest is Providence. The exemplary function of the Heartfrees is thus to recommend virtue and innocence, but not as an imitable counter to evil machinations and impositions. The Heartfrees are certainly not condemned, yet they make an indirect contribution to the temporary success of villainy by being so gullible. Innocence can only be armed against hypocrisy if hypocrisy is exposed, but innocence has no means of overcoming hypocrisy.

Fielding pays the usual price for the generalising tendency of his satire: his allegorical characterisation is simple to the point of crudity. His are not the characters we are accustomed to expect in novels: they look as if they belong more aptly in a morality play. Laetitia Snap, Bagshot, Fireblood, Friendly, Smirk, even the Heartfrees, are barely more than ciphers whose actions alone are enough to confirm the implications of their names. Even Wild himself is only an extended caricature. Fielding's narrator is 'content' to describe Fireblood 'negatively' by 'telling our reader what qualities he had not; in which number were humanity, modesty, and fear, not one grain of any of which was mingled in his whole composition' (III, 4). If Fielding's characters ever surprise us, it is because of the dramatic configurations in which we find them. Thus, in the best tradition of theatrical farce, Laetitia rejects Wild's amorous advances because Tom Smirk is waiting in her closet (I, 9–10). Once we know this, we know why she behaves as she does. (Wild never finds out.) Generally, her behaviour is predictable and consistent: thus her character is not developed and so not really very interesting, but it perfectly exemplifies Fielding's theatrical characterisation:

This young lady, among many other good ingredients, had three very predominant passions; to wit, vanity, wantonness, and avarice. To satisfy the first of these she employed Mr Smirk and company; to the second, Mr Bagshot and company; and our hero had the honour and happiness of solely engrossing the third. Now, these three sorts of lovers she had very different ways of entertaining. With the first she was all gay and coquette; with the second all fond and rampant; and with the last all cold and reserved. (II, 3)

Similarly, like all great men, Wild exercises perfect control over the facial muscles (II, 3). Indeed he is primarily an actor, as we learn in the revealing scene where he is alone in a boat: professing his readiness to die fearlessly, 'he looked extremely fierce, but, recollecting that no one was present to see him, he relaxed the terror of his countenance, and, pausing a while, repeated the last word, "D—n!" ' (II, 11). He is similarly theatrical when he employs his 'usual method' of leaving a tavern without paying a bill: 'cocking his hat fiercely, he marched out of the room without making any excuse, or any one daring to make the least demand' (II, 4). Facial expressions are stylised in the manner of stage directions to suggest abstracted emotion or gesture, rather than part of a developed, naturalistic character. Fielding gives us only what we need to know: and we do not need to know, say, how long a character's nose is, what shape the face, or what colour the eyes. Since all the thieves and whores maintain appearances belied by their actions, and thus speak of honour and honesty while robbing one another, they are all actors. Also, two chapters take the form of theatrical dialogues, and two further hints suggest that Fielding's conception of his narrative is theatrical. He takes up the commonplace comparison of the world and the stage to point out one difference. In the theatre

the hero or chief figure is almost continually before your eyes, whilst the under-actors are not seen above once in an evening; now, on the [stage of the world], the hero or great man is always behind the curtain, and seldom or never appears or doth anything in his own person. He doth indeed, in this GRAND DRAMA, rather perform the part of the prompter, and doth instruct the well-drest figures, who are strutting in public on the stage, what to say and do. To say the truth, a puppet-show will illustrate our meaning better, where it is the master of the show (the great man) who dances and moves everything . . . but he himself keeps wisely out of sight . . .   (III, 11)

This interesting comment raises an important point. The real 'great man' – Walpole, Alexander, Julius Caesar – is the puppet-master in this image; in Pope's parallel conception, 'as the Prompter breathes, the Puppet squeaks'. But Wild is continually before our eyes in Fielding's novel and, far from manipulating, Wild is constantly manipulated: he is the puppet, not the prompter. Wild's prompter can be none but the author, who elsewhere attributes his function to Nature, Fortune, or Providence. Thus, the more Wild is idealised, the more contemptible an example of greatness he is. If he is ridiculous, so is greatness. All these elements come together at the end. As the whole story draws to a close, Fielding laments that Fortune all too often,

like a lazy poet, winds up her catastrophe awkwardly, and, bestowing too little care on her fifth act, dismisses the hero with a sneaking and private exit, who had in the former part of the drama performed such notable exploits as must promise to every good judge among the spectators a noble, public, and exalted end.

But she was resolved to commit no such error in this instance.   (IV, 14)

Wild's 'noble, public, and exalted end', arranged 'in this instance' by the author, is of course to be hanged. These theatrical elements of the novel account for the crudity of Fielding's characterisation and are essential to create the gap between the real and the ironic ideal.

Since the great world that Fielding represents is a 'GRAND DRAMA', it is appropriate that *Jonathan Wild* should employ dramatic techniques. But it is not drama, it is a novel with a narrator. The authorial voice reminds us of what we are reading and how we should interpret what we read. Directly descended from Hercules Vinegar, the narrator is perhaps Fielding's most important innovation in *Wild*. While the narrator provides the basis of the mock-heroic incongruity and irony that sustain the entire book, he is also the apparently normative figure through whom the satirist's judgment is expressed.

The narrator frequently pauses to address his 'more sagacious readers, whose satisfaction we shall always consult in the most especial manner' (II, 8); to appeal to the reader's experience (I, 14); to assume a common attitude shared by his readers and himself (I, 14); to clear up a doubtful point (II, 1); to explain why a scene

41

is included 'for the amusement of six or seven readers only' (II, 9); or to justify a digression about 'how apt men are to hate those they injure' (III, 4):

> As we scorn to keep any discoveries secret from our readers, whose instruction, as well as diversion, we have greatly considered in this history, we have here digressed somewhat to communicate the following short lesson to those who are simple and well inclined: though as a Christian thou art obliged, and we advise thee, to forgive thy enemy, NEVER TRUST THE MAN WHO HATH REASON TO SUSPECT THAT YOU KNOW HE HATH INJURED YOU. (III, 4)

All these instances develop a relationship between 'author' and 'reader'. The 'author' is thus truthful and candid, being obliged 'to preserve the fidelity of our history' (I, 10). The implied reader is drawn into a sort of conspiracy with this ingenuous 'author': Wild opens a casket 'and took forth (with sorrow I write it, and with sorrow will it be read) one of those beautiful necklaces which, at the fair of Bartholomew, they deck the well-bewhitened neck of Thalestris Queen of the Amazons, Anna Bullen, Queen Elizabeth, or some other high princess of Drollic story' (II, 3). At this point, Wild seems to have betrayed the principles of greatness by passing off paste costume jewellery used by street entertainers as if it were the real thing. But the joke is not over yet: the fakes have been substituted by Molly Straddle. The mock-sorrow comes about, therefore, because Wild has been duped by his whore, and because he cannot tell the difference between real stones and paste, while Molly can, and Laetitia, who is about to fly into a rage, also can. The mock-sorrow is confidently attributed to the writer *and to the reader*. This ingenuousness is very obviously a formal device, which reminds us that the narrative is consciously and deliberately constructed. We can never think of the narrator as the author, since there is too great a moral distance between the condemnation of great men's exploits and the narrator's determination to celebrate them. While the 'author' is at pains to tell us that his narrative is 'natural' – that is, he has no recourse to the 'prodigious' solutions of romance – he simultaneously shows us that it is unnatural, by being artificial. When Heartfree has been reprieved and a surgeon called in to Newgate to bleed everyone concerned, a new chapter begins:

> But here, though I am convinced my good-natured reader may almost want the surgeon's assistance also, and that there is no passage in this whole story which can afford him equal delight, yet, lest our reprieve should seem to resemble that in the *Beggar's Opera*, I shall endeavour to shew him that this incident, which is undoubtedly true, is at least as natural as delightful; for

we assure him we would rather have suffered half mankind to be hanged, than have saved one contrary to the strictest rules of writing and probability. (IV, 6)

Thus, what the 'author' calls 'natural' is no more than an authorial convention. The 'author' is therefore the vehicle of mock-heroic: he introduces the ludicrously inappropriate mock-epic similes; he controls the disparity between the heroic language and unheroic characters: he even confesses that 'the historian' always 'embellishes the diction with some flourishes of his own eloquence' (III, 6). The ironic intent of *Jonathan Wild* demands linguistic incongruity as the basic tone of the narrative. Thus in his parody of the propitious circumstances of the hero's birth, Fielding is playing a game with us; he gives us seemingly innocent descriptions involving hints and clues that we must interpret. To give one small example: 'Some say his mother was delivered of him in an house of an orbicular or round form in Covent Garden; but of this we are not certain' (I, 3). 'Orbicular' is a conspicuously inappropriate adjective to allude to a round-house, or prison. In the same fashion, we decode the narrative to learn that Wild is the son of a thieving whore. Also, with the same professed uncertainty, this narrator habitually raises points whose issue he cannot or will not 'determine'; he is tentative in speaking of the relation between Wild and Laetitia, 'for though, being his cousin-german, she was *perhaps*, in the eye of a strict conscience, somewhat too nearly related to him, yet the old people on both sides, though sufficiently scrupulous in nice matters, agreed to overlook this objection' (I, 4; my italics). The effect of 'perhaps' is quite the opposite of the tentativeness it appears to convey, so that without any difficulty we can see the clear moral judgment that lies behind the words of the 'author'.

Such understatement is sham coyness, which, as the narrative unfolds, becomes the characteristic tone of the 'author'. Bagshot, for instance, 'had inadvertently departed' from his lodgings 'without taking a formal leave' and is now arrested (II, 11). Only the 'author' attributes inadvertency to Bagshot. The expression tells us literally that Bagshot forgot to say goodbye to his landlady. No one is fooled by this; underneath the exterior of polite behaviour suggested by these words, is the contrary image of a petty crook running off without paying his rent. The ironic incongruity of the narrator's words continually draws attention in this way to the disparity between the literal and rhetorical connotations of language. Thus the language that usually describes a young gentleman's Grand Tour describes Wild's transportation as a criminal to the American plantations (I, 7). The disparity constantly forces the 'sagacious reader' to recognise a difference between what people do and what they say – or, ultimately, between what they are and what they seem to be.

It is not only the 'author' who fails to see the differences. The thieves also adopt a code of social behaviour, which dictates that they – as doggedly as the narrator – call one another gentlemen, and so on.

Indeed it may appear strange to some readers that these gentlemen, who knew each other to be thieves, should never once give the least hint of this knowledge in all their discourse together, but, on the contrary, should have the words honesty, honour, and friendship as often in their mouths as any other men. This, I say, may appear strange to some; but those who have lived long in cities, courts, gaols, or such places, will perhaps be able to solve the seeming absurdity. (I, 6)

The words are in their mouths, it is true, but are never translated into honest, honourable, or friendly actions: those are the province of the Heartfrees, who are therefore objects of scorn and contempt in Newgate. In the 'great' world of 'cities, courts, gaols, or such places', which are governed by hypocrisy, a Thomas Heartfree will have to learn the hard way: because 'He was of that sort of men whom experience only, and not their own natures, must inform that there are such things as deceit and hypocrisy in the world' (II, 1). One means of survival is to learn to recognise hypocrisy, which nobody does very well in *Wild*. Another is to act on the assumption that everyone is hypocritical: all the thieves and whores take this option, and thus try to stay one jump ahead of their rivals. The gullible Heartfree has to learn by experience that words must be supported by actions.

In a telling episode the 'author' accounts for Wild's return to the boat in which he has been set adrift. Wild is declaiming:

'Let a pack of cowardly rascals be afraid of death, I dare look him in the face. But shall I stay and be starved? – No, I will eat up the biscuits the French son of a whore bestowed on me, and then leap into the sea for drink, since the unconscionable dog hath not allowed me a single dram.' Having thus said, he proceeded immediately to put his purpose in execution, and, as his resolution never failed him, he had no sooner dispatched the small quantity of provision which his enemy had with no vast liberality presented him, than he cast himself headlong into the sea . . .

Now, Nature having originally intended our great man for that final exaltation which, as it is the most proper and becoming end of all great men, it were heartily to be wished they might all arrive at, would by no means be diverted from her purpose. She, therefore, no sooner spied him in the water than she softly whispered in his ear to attempt the recovery of his boat, which call he immediately obeyed, and, being a good swimmer, and it being a perfect calm, with great facility accomplished it.   (II, 11–12)

Wild's actions do not match his words. If they did, his return to the boat would have to be achieved by 'a supernatural agent'. A genuine hero does match his words with actions. Wild himself, in one of his entirely incongruous formal speeches, recognises the relationship between words, actions, and 'honour':

A man of honour is he that is called a man of honour; and while he is so called he so remains, and no longer. Think not anything a man commits can forfeit his honour. Look abroad into the world; the PRIG, while he flourishes, is a man of honour; when in gaol, at the bar, or the tree, he is so no longer. And why is this distinction? Not from his actions; for those are often as well known in his flourishing estate as they are afterwards; but because men, I mean those of his own party or gang, call him a man of honour in the former, and cease to call him so in the latter condition.   (I, 13)

This is not merely a swipe at hypocrisy, nor merely a dig at a politician who breaks his word. Because language is so corrupted that men never need mean what they say or do what they promise, evil is certain to prosper. Such linguistic corruption, at the heart of Fielding's mock-heroic style, thus conceals true motives. One central question about greatness is what makes a man great: Wild's answer, here, is that a man is great when someone says he is. It is not the great alone who are corrupt: those who call evil men great are equally corrupt, and perhaps therefore equally guilty. Those who do so are the man's 'own party or gang': a political party or a gang of criminals or the biographers. The concept of linguistic corruption is again brought back into the political context. The structure of politics – the very language of political discourse – allows the innocent to be hoodwinked by men who pose as 'honourable', 'virtuous', 'good', and 'great'. Unless they are warned the innocent will be deceived or destroyed. *Jonathan Wild* provides the warning.

3

Shamela and *Joseph Andrews*

Samuel Richardson's first novel, *Pamela: or, Virtue Rewarded* was published in November 1740. It was a triumph, a sensation. Perpetually tinkering with his text, Richardson brought out four revised editions in less than a year. He soon added a sequel (*Pamela in her Exalted Condition*) and later virtually rewrote the whole novel twice more. *Pamela* had also provoked other writers to take up their pens. Like most literary triumphs, this novel was subjected to spurious sequels, adaptations, imitations, and parodies. One of the parodists was Fielding, who hated *Pamela* with a passion. Five months after the first appearance of Richardson's long novel, Fielding reacted with a short pamphlet, *An Apology for the Life of Mrs Shamela Andrews*, better known as *Shamela*. For a short time this too was popular, but it seems to have chagrined Richardson and his circle of friends, which later included Fielding's sister Sarah. Like its ostensible model, *Shamela* was published anonymously. The story goes that when Fielding discovered the authorship of *Pamela*, he regretted the offence his parody had caused; whether or not this was the reason, Fielding never publicly admitted that he had written *Shamela*.

Among the earliest novels seriously to develop the form of letters written by the characters, *Pamela* had appeared at a time when the novel – in any form – was still not secure in the literary market place. Richardson found an audience among the growing middle classes, who valued his narrative, for *Pamela* embodies an essentially middle-class morality. Pamela Andrews, a servant-girl, resists the advances of her seducer, the wealthy squire Mr B., until he does the right thing by her; that is, until he marries her. While the seduction takes place, Pamela finds she loves him in spite of herself, and Mr B. eventually values her resistance so highly that he falls in love with her. Pamela's 'virtue' is equivalent to her virginity, her urgent desire to preserve it no more than prudent self-interest. If the novel turns on a matter of principle, it is that virginity pays. It is this central element of *Pamela* that Fielding exposes in *Shamela*.

Although not great literature, *Shamela* is interesting, especially as a forerunner of *Joseph Andrews*. Fielding's method is burlesque: his narrative imitates Richardson's epistolary style – even down to the letters between the supposed discoverer of the original manuscripts and the clergyman to whom he sends them. In Fielding's treatment, Richardson's almost saintly servant becomes a cunning, shameless minx; her virtue is corrupted into 'vartue'; with a delicious irony, Mr B.'s full name is discovered to be Booby; Pamela's prudent self-interest is also Shamela's, but where Pamela's reward is her exalted condition, Shamela is satisfied with money. Shamela, the sham, is the epitome of pretence, hypocrisy, and greed, always with an eye to the main chance. The wealthy squire is on the way to impoverishment by his bride once she recognises the power of her upgraded status: having asked him for a hundred guineas two days running, Shamela declares: 'I believe I shall buy every Thing I see. What signifies having Money if one doth not spend it[?].' She demands another hundred the next day, at which Booby asks how she could have spent so much so fast; her reply: 'Truly, says I, Sir, I shall live like other Ladies of my Fashion; and if you think, because I was a Servant, that I shall be contented to be governed as you please, I will shew you, you are mistaken.' She then fakes a fainting fit, deflects his questions, and receives the money: 'I fancy I have effectually prevented any farther Refusals or Inquiry into my Expences. It would be hard indeed that a Woman who marries a Man only for his Money should be debarred from spending it' (348–9).

As that episode reveals, Shamela is callous and cynical, so much so that she is content to disown her mother on the grounds that her own new social status is now too high to allow her to be seen with one of so low a rank. Yet *Shamela* is not carping and bitter: although it is a serious attack on the morality of *Pamela*, it is also a very funny parody. A little nasty perhaps, Shamela's cynicism itself can be an object of fun:

The most difficult Task for me was to blush; however, by holding my Breath, and squeezing my Cheeks with my Handkerchief, I did pretty well . . . Well, at last I went to Bed, and my Husband soon leapt in after me; where I shall only assure you, I acted my Part in such a manner, that no Bridegroom was ever better satisfied with his Bride's Virginity.   (347)

Both the theatricality of Shamela's manufactured blush and her success in taking in the gullible Squire Booby, provoke laughter, even if it is tinged with scorn. Possibly the most quoted paragraph of the whole piece is one of Shamela's ludicrous descriptions of a nocturnal visit from Booby (before their marriage):

Thursday Night, Twelve o'Clock

Mrs. *Jervis* and I are just in Bed, and the Door unlocked; if my Master should come – Odsbobs! I hear him just coming in at the Door. You see I write in the present Tense, as Parson *Williams* says. Well, he is in Bed between us, we both shamming a Sleep, he steals his Hand into my Bosom, which I, as if in my Sleep, press close to me with mine, and then pretend to awake. – I no sooner see him, but I scream out . . .   (330)

By so absurdly emphasising the present tense for a spurious immediacy, this passage sends up Richardson's narrative technique of having Pamela write 'to the moment'; but the passage can also stand on its own as sardonic wit. Some isolated passages in *Shamela* are not at all dependent on *Pamela* for their effect. When Shamela sits in her husband's carriage listening to her lover, Parson Williams, she responds in a way that provokes our laughter and draws attention not to *Pamela* explicitly so much as the morality which Shamela has come to represent:

Therefore, says he, my Dear, you have two Husbands, one the Object of your Love, and to satisfy your Desire; the other the Object of your Necessity, and to furnish you with those other Conveniences. (I am sure I remember every Word, for he repeated it three Times; O he is very good whenever I desire him to repeat a thing to me three Times he always doth it!) as then the Spirit is preferable to the Flesh, so am I preferable to your other Husband, to whom I am antecedent in Time likewise. I say these things, my Dear, (said he) to satisfie your Conscience. A Fig for my Conscience, said I, when shall I meet you again in the Garden?   (351)

The bawdiness of Shamela's interpolation anticipates her easy dismissal of matters spiritual. It is clear, then, that she cares not a fig for Pamela's type of virtue.

There is more satire at Richardson's expense. The slightly obsessive accumulation of apparently trivial detail creates a minutely portrayed world in *Pamela*. Fielding's parody shows how easily such detail can become an end in itself, and so be arbitrary, inconsequential, and superfluous:

Mrs. *Jewkes* went in with me, and helped me to pack up my little All, which was soon done; being no more than two Day-Caps, two Night-Caps, five

Shifts, one Sham, a Hoop, a Quilted-Petticoat, two Flannel-Petticoats, two pair of Stockings, one odd one, a pair of lac'd Shoes, a short flowered Apron, a lac'd Neck-Handkerchief, one Clog, and almost another, and some few Books: as, *A full Answer to a plain and true Account*, &c. *The Whole Duty of Man*, with only the Duty to one's Neighbour, torn out. The Third Volume of the *Atalantis*. *Venus in the Cloyster: Or, the Nun in her Smock. God's Dealings with Mr. Whitefield. Orfus and Eurydice.* Some Sermon-Books; and two or three Plays, with their Titles, and Part of the first Act torn off. (344)

Not only is this list absurdly haphazard, it also indicates something of Fielding's broader aims: the books include mild pornography, a volume on Methodist doctrine, and a much read devotional book, *The Whole Duty of Man.* But it is noticeable that Shamela's copy of this last does not include the part about duty to one's neighbour, so that her self-interest is represented even by a book in her motley library. *Venus in the Cloyster* is one of many pointers to a feature of Fielding's whole parody that must have offended Richardson and can sometimes offend modern readers: the bawdy. The language of *Shamela* is peppered (as Fielding would say) with slang, much of it now obsolete and obscure, *double entendre*, and plain obscenity. Fielding's prurient innuendo coarsens Richardson's 'moral' tale by turning it into a thinly disguised lascivious adventure. Richardson's reader is thus endowed – in Fielding's treatment – with the mentality of a voyeur.

My emphasis lies on *Shamela*'s nature as a destructive satiric weapon. Fielding lets it go at that, in the sense that he does not construct any serious alternative to the hypocrisy he evidently loathed. But *Shamela* is not aimed at *Pamela* alone. Fielding also attacks the Methodism of George Whitefield, the moral corruption of the clergy, Lord Hervey (one of the most prominent courtiers of the day), the author Conyers Middleton, and the actor and playwright, Colley Cibber.

Whitefield is singled out for propagating a doctrine that offers a specious, conscience-salving form of words that covers as it encourages immorality. Parson Williams' sermon

shewed us that the Bible doth not require too much Goodness of us, and that People very often call things Goodness that are not so. That to go to Church, and to pray, and to sing Psalms, and to honour the Clergy, and to repent, is true Religion; and 'tis not doing good to one another, for that is one of the greatest Sins we can commit, when we don't do it for the sake of Religion. That those People who talk of Vartue and Morality, are the wickedest of all Persons. That 'tis not what we do, but what we believe, that must save us . . . (336)

The moral corruption of the clergy is obvious enough not only in this pernicious doctrine attributed to the Methodists and in the dubious character and conduct of Parson Williams, but also in Parson Tickletext. Tickletext fulsomely recommends *Shamela* to his fellow clergyman, Parson Oliver, in the first letter. Tickletext has 'done nothing but read it to others, and hear others again read it to me', and his neighbouring clergymen have 'made it our common Business here, not only to cry it up, but to preach it up likewise'. As his admiration increases, the satire begins to take shape: Tickletext exclaims, 'Happy would it be for Mankind, if all other Books were burnt, that we might do nothing but read thee all Day, and dream of thee all Night' (322). Once we have recognised the bawdy hints that follow, we know what kind of dreams those will be. He continues: 'Thou alone art sufficient to teach us as much Morality as we want' but not, one supposes, as much as the clergy should have. Then turning his attention to the author, Tickletext adds: 'The Comprehensiveness of his Imagination must be truly prodigious! It has stretched out this diminutive mere Grain of Mustard-Seed (a poor Girl's little, *&c.*) into a Resemblance of that Heaven, which the best of good Books has compared it to' (322). Distorting Richardson's original phrase, 'a poor Girl's little, innocent Story', the bawdy ambiguity strikes simultaneously at both the lecherous clergy and the vulgar author, for these two sentences are direct quotations from Richardson.

The dedicatory epistle 'To Miss *Fanny*, *&c*' establishes Fielding's satirical thrusts at Cibber, Middleton, and Hervey. Few readers now will recognise the allusions, for few now know that 'Lord Fanny' was a common pejorative nickname for the effeminate and allegedly hermaphrodite (a contemporary term for homosexual) Lord Hervey. Few now will realise that Fielding's epistle is verbally very close to Middleton's dedication – to Hervey – of his *History of the Life of Marcus Tullius Cicero*, actually quite a respectable biography. Cibber will be a familiar name to readers of Fielding's drama or of Pope's *Dunciad* of 1743. However, 'Conny Keyber' (that is, 'Conyers' plus 'Cibber'), the 'author' of the epistle dedicatory – in fact, according to the title page the alleged author of *Shamela* – may be puzzling. The full title of *Shamela* actually recalls Cibber's recently published, controversial *Apology for the Life of Mr Colley Cibber*, an autobiography whose appalling English and incredible vanity Fielding had already attacked in the *Champion* and would attack again, with more telling effect, in *Joseph Andrews*. To anyone with no knowledge of Cibber (impossible ignorance amongst the literati of London in 1741), the alignment of Cibber with Richardson will pass unnoticed. Similarly, the inclusion of Hervey as one of the satiric victims introduces a political dimension which is now generally accessible only to the specialist. Fielding's protests against these people are all aimed, one way or another, against corruption – moral, political, and linguistic – but all the protests rely on knowledge that *Shamela* itself does not generally provide. *Shamela*, then, may offer serious criticism and a good deal of fun, but it is too topical to take a place alongside the lasting satires of the age: *Shamela* is dated, as spoofs usually are.

On 22 February 1742, less than a year after the first appearance of *Shamela*, two small volumes were published under the title *The History of the Adventures of Joseph Andrews, and of his Friend Mr. Abraham Adams. Written in Imitation of Cervantes, Author of Don Quixote*. This much loved novel is a far wider and more deeply developed response to *Pamela*, but this time Fielding did offer a serious alternative to the corruption, hypocrisy, greed, and self-interest he had hit so hard in *Shamela*. *Joseph Andrews* is also based on a number of models with which (regrettably) comparatively few modern readers are familiar: the Bible (for the story of Joseph and Potiphar's wife), *Don Quixote*, and the *Odyssey*. But although these models account for the structure of the narrative and suggest the underlying virtue of the two principal characters, they are transcended in Fielding's rich mixture of satire and comedy.

Joseph Andrews himself, 'brother to the illustrious Pamela', is a footman in the service of Sir Thomas Booby, uncle of Pamela's Mr B. Sir Thomas is quickly and casually dispatched, dying off early in the novel: 'his disconsolate lady' recovers so quickly from the shock that within seven days she is trying to seduce the incredibly virtuous Joseph, whom she angrily discharges for resisting her amorous attempts. She invents a different charge against him, accusing him, with grotesque injustice, of sexual licentiousness. In this Lady Booby is abetted by her equally voracious but astonishingly ugly waiting-gentlewoman, Mrs Slipslop. Since they recall *Pamela* so explicitly, the early chapters, describing the seduction and Joseph's relationship with Pamela, suggest that *Joseph Andrews* will continue Fielding's war on *Pamela*.

The brief first chapter of Book I seems to promise something built on a response to Cibber's *Apology* and *Pamela*. Fielding distinguishes himself from these authors in two ways. Firstly, where Cibber brazenly portrayed himself, and Richardson posed only as the editor of others' correspondence, Fielding adopts the role of the historian or biographer who records what the participants have told him afterwards about their adventures. He therefore professes neither total detachment nor total involvement. Cibber's book, he says,

> was written by the great Person himself, who lived the Life he hath recorded, and is by many thought to have lived such a Life only in order to write it. The other is communicated to us by an Historian who borrows his Lights, as the common Method is, from authentic Papers and Records. (I, i)

When Coleridge likened Richardson to a stuffy, hot sick-room, and Fielding to an open lawn on a breezy day, he identified a distinction that Fielding made himself, in a way. Fielding's objections to *Pamela* include his distaste for epistolary fiction and in particular the claustrophobic, introverted nature of a story told in this way: hence *Shamela*'s parody of the obsessive heaping up of detail, even the parody of letters *per se*, hints at the author's desire to break out from the suffocation of Richardson's enclosed world. In a corresponding way, Cibber's self-indulgent autobiography is the epitome of vanity, or unhealthy enclosure of another kind, in which Cibber occupies the centre of a stage from which all others are excluded. In *Joseph Andrews* Fielding carefully dissociates himself from both these modes of telling a story. Fielding's own chosen narrative mode is to install an amiable, talkative narrator who engages his reader in what amounts to a social act, something akin to conversation. It is as if the author throws open the doors of his home to let in both the air and us, his visitors.

A second way in which Fielding dissociates himself from Cibber and Richardson is by stressing virtue as his subject, contrasting with Richardson's 'Virtue Rewarded' – and we have seen what *Shamela* does with that – and Cibber's 'Male-Virtue', which is not virtue at all:

> The authentic History with which I now present the public, is an Instance of the great good that Book [*Pamela*] is likely to do, and of the Prevalence of Example . . . since it will appear that it was by keeping the excellent Pattern of his Sister's Virtues before his Eyes, that Mr. *Joseph Andrews* was chiefly enabled to preserve his Purity in the midst of such great Temptations; I shall only add, that this Character of Male-Chastity, tho' doubtless as desirable and becoming in one Part of the human Species, as in the other, is almost the only Virtue which the great Apologist [that is, Cibber] hath not given himself for the sake of giving the Example to his Readers. (I, i)

The concepts of history, examples, and virtue will be important later, but here, at the end of the first chapter, they are subordinate to Fielding's joke, which reminds us that he imitates neither of his 'models'. Pamela and her husband themselves appear in Book IV of

Joseph Andrews: although Pamela has little to say there, she still manages to condemn herself. But by introducing Pamela and Mr B., Fielding brings his characters together in a comic dénouement (which develops into a travesty of *Oedipus*), simultaneously offering a satirical commentary on the bourgeois values embraced by Richardson. Pamela and Mr B. try to persuade Joseph that he must forsake his beloved Fanny, a milkmaid, because such a match would damage the Booby family's social status, Pamela herself notwithstanding. The concealed reason for this sudden snobbery is that Lady Booby still wants Joseph to herself to satisfy her carnal desires. The novel is brought to an end with another gibe at Richardson, but by then most readers are unlikely to be concerned with specific allusions to either *Pamela* or Cibber's *Apology*. Although jokes and satirical thrusts directed at Richardson and Cibber are scattered through the narrative, they neither dominate nor give shape to *Joseph Andrews* in the sense that they do *Shamela*. For although the writings of these two men are symptomatic of evils which Fielding saw as menacing social and individual virtue, *Joseph Andrews* has more substantial matter to offer than a riposte to two books. It is most rewarding to approach *Joseph Andrews* through its dramatised conflicts between virtue and vice; its exposure of affectation and vanity in the light of Fielding's expressed aims; its narrative technique; Fielding's satiric conception of character and of the famous 'comic Epic-Poem in Prose'. Together with these elements, Fielding's characterisation reveals the two dominant themes of the novel: chastity and charity, the one an expression of individual, the other of social, virtue. In *Joseph Andrews* Fielding creates an ironic, and finally more realistic, alternative to the Richardsonian novel.

II

Despite Fielding's relentless portrayal of evil dramatised, *Joseph Andrews* remains a good-humoured novel. The agent of good humour is one of Fielding's most delightful creations, Parson Abraham Adams. Always at the centre of the comedy, Adams, rather than Joseph, is the hero of the novel and one who commands our affection from the first. The shabby, mud-stained parson, his cassock always torn and slipping, his wig hanging off his head, his beard a 'piss-burnt' colour after one particularly messy adventure, Adams always springs to the defence of the defenceless, without ever considering the consequences of his action. With his formidable classical learning, the absent-minded parson thinks he knows the world, but the adventures continually reveal that he keeps finding precisely the opposite of what he expects. Adams takes people at face value, for he is able to see in others only what they let him see. He therefore trusts the untrustworthy and believes the promises of liars and hypocrites. If vices are personified in mean innkeepers, hypocritical fashionable ladies and their snooty servants, and self-centred clergymen, virtue is personified in the lovable Adams through all his scrapes. Virtue, as we shall see, is an active principle.

Like Charlie Chaplin recovering from every setback by outwitting the bully, Adams repeatedly regains his dignity after temporary defeats to emerge victorious. It is in Adams that almost all the positive values of the novel have their origin; and the interaction of Adams with other characters provides the novel's focus of attention once Joseph has been dismissed from Lady Booby's service. Indeed, the sheer exuberance of Adams is the main source of the novel's entertainment, but in good neoclassical fashion Fielding intended to convey instruction as well as entertainment. Besides aiming to please, Fielding aimed, with more seriousness, to expose hypocrisy and uncharitableness. As the active opponent of the vices Fielding seeks to expose, Adams is the main source of 'instruction' too.

In his preface, Fielding outlines his principal subject:

The only Source of the true Ridiculous (as it appears to me) is Affectation . . . Now Affectation proceeds from one of these two Causes, Vanity, or Hypocrisy: for as Vanity puts us on affecting false Characters, in order to purchase Applause; so Hypocrisy sets us on an Endeavour to avoid Censure by concealing our Vices under an Appearance of their opposite Virtues . . .

From the Discovery of this Affectation arises the Ridiculous – which always strikes the Reader with Surprize and Pleasure; and that in a higher and stronger Degree when the Affectation arises from Hypocrisy, than when from Vanity: for to discover any one to be the exact Reverse of what he affects, is more surprizing, and consequently more ridiculous, than to find him a little deficient in the Quality he desires Reputation of.

Fielding's stated domain is related to those of the best-known Augustan satires – *Gulliver's Travels*, *The Dunciad*, *The Beggar's Opera* – albeit on a smaller scale. To expose vanity and hypocrisy, an ability to raise laughter is more appropriate than sombreness of tone. In *Joseph Andrews*, from the jauntiness of the preface until the last page, laughter is more in evidence than sombreness, especially where Parson Adams is concerned. If he is to achieve his aim, Fielding must engage his reader's sympathy (which may explain

F. R. Leavis' sneer that Fielding was a mere rhetorician without depth of moral insight). By making us laugh and by winning our affection for his simple, impulsive, and naive generosity, Adams engages our sympathy. The vices of those he opposes are thus the more detestable, and the more effectively exposed by the contrast.

In exposing vices, Fielding places great emphasis on individual examples and incidents, but little on a complex plot structure (although *Joseph Andrews* is more carefully structured than it seems). Because the plot does not seem to be a tightly controlled entity, but appears to be only a series of adventures loosely held together by the journey motif, *Joseph Andrews* is sometimes called – erroneously – a picaresque novel (from '*pícaro*' – a rogue). There are in *Joseph Andrews* superficial resemblances to picaresque fiction, but the only novel that Fielding was consciously imitating was *Don Quixote*. Proclaimed on the title page of *Joseph Andrews*, Fielding's conscious debt to Cervantes explains why the plot consists of adventures on the road. Correspondences between Parson Adams and Don Quixote have been noticed before. Without believing that country inns are enchanted castles, Adams resembles Quixote in that both are innocents in a hostile world, and in their different ways both are deluded. Adams, for instance, is so unworldly that he expects an innkeeper to accept a volume of sermons as security for a loan to pay the bill. The more serious, structural correspondences between *Joseph Andrews* and *Don Quixote* reveal in Fielding's novel an affinity with the ambiguous satiric comedy of Cervantes. Like Cervantes, Fielding accumulates separate scenes, populated mostly by rogues of one sort or another, but with occasional friendly characters also crossing the travellers' path; there are bills to be paid, somehow, and battles to be fought, and beds to be slept in by the right people; each scene brings new problems to be solved, new obstacles to be overcome. Fielding's method effectively portrays the variety of human experience, while also enabling the novel to create representative examples of the vices it exposes.

Instead of unfolding a particularly complex pattern of events, Fielding creates a relatively simple world where the passage of time (less than a fortnight, if we count) and the total course of action are unimportant. The major characters live from one day to the next, walking home through the English countryside, stopping at inns, meeting brutish country squires and boorish, pompous clergymen, conversing with fellow travellers, and running out of money. The abiding image of the world of *Joseph Andrews* is not of Booby Hall but of muddy roads and travel-stained greatcoats, horses and stagecoaches, cosy parlours and wood fires, mugs of ale and plates of cold roast beef. This world is where real life is lived, or so Fielding invites us to believe. In a familiar Augustan formulation derived from such classical authors as Horace and Juvenal, the rural environment itself contains values opposed to those of the city. In this polarity the city is the home of artificiality and 'fashion', while the country is more natural. Although neither is perfect, the country is preferable. The city, which corrupts the externals of Joseph's conduct, but the morals of most others, is carried over into Booby Hall, since Lady Booby's 'Town-Education' encourages her to speak of 'her Country Neighbours' as *'The Brutes'* (I, iii). The contrast is clear in Book IV, which distinguishes between the cynical meanness of the owner of Booby Hall on her return from London and the attractive benevolence of Adams in his humble country cottage. The contrast is repeated as the action shifts from one to the other. The dichotomy between country and city is expressed in this and in a series of parallel individual contrasts – between the natural and the artificial, the virtuous and the evil, the charitable and the uncharitable, the naive and the sophisticated. In Fielding's comic resolution victory is finally awarded to the innocent and virtuous. The vicious are simply dismissed. Similarly, the conduct of the innocent victims of individual incidents in the country constitutes a slightly exaggerated portrait of vibrant but natural life, in contrast with the artifice and insincerity of fashionable society. The separate elements of Fielding's fiction together expose the ridiculous: the affected, or vain and hypocritical.

At a symbolic level, the individual adventures, and what the travellers can learn from them, are considerably more important than any overall design that we would normally think of as a plot. Yet the apparent shapelessness of the plot is revealing. Like the lives of the Heartfrees in *Jonathan Wild*, the lives of these characters seem to be governed by Providence, for the plot develops according to what Providence lays in store for them from scene to scene and inn to inn. Important in itself, the role of Providence helps to illuminate Fielding's conception of a controlling, omniscient author, through whose judgment the entire narrative passes and through whom the satire is sharply focused.

As Maynard Mack has noted in his introduction to *Joseph Andrews*, our point of view must be continuous with the author's, not the characters'; our laughter is the laughter of onlookers. In a plot where connections between events seem superficial and accidental, the role of Providence draws attention to the hairsbreadth escapes, the coincidental meetings and their consequent revelations; it also draws attention to the idea of a presiding force. As onlookers, we can see that the author is that presiding force: he acts the part of Providence.

Providence is what Adams claims to live by. When Fanny makes her first appearance in the novel, she is about to be raped, as usual, but Adams rescues her. Since they do not recognise one another in the pitch dark of night, she is still afraid. In the first of two parallel incidents later, Fanny is delivered from the hands of one ravisher into those of another, Peter Pounce, and in the second she is rescued by Joseph from the attentions of Beau Didapper. These incidents typify a pattern in which the innocents, Adams, Joseph, and Fanny, are thrown back on their own resources to combat the continual threats of the forces of evil. In each of these three cases, where Fanny's chastity is rescued in the nick of time, what seems accidental is actually providential.

When Adams has rescued Fanny from her first assailant, she explains that she had 'put her whole Trust in Providence, and walk'd on' with the man, but he soon 'was attempting to execute his wicked Will' when Adams arrived: '*Adams* encouraged her for saying, she had put her whole Trust in Providence, and told her "he doubted not but Providence had sent him to her Deliverance, as a Reward for that Trust"' (II, ix). He urges her to continue to 'repose thy Trust in the same Providence, which hath hitherto protected thee, and never will forsake the Innocent' (II, x), a statement which is proved true by the resolution of the plot. Later, upon hearing a voice in the dark speaking of murder, Adams 'committed himself to the care of Providence' (III, ii) since, as he explains later to Joseph, 'no Accident happens to us without the Divine Permission, and it is the Duty of a Man, much more of a Christian, to submit' (III, xi). For all that he professes resignation to Divine Providence, Adams is no more capable of submission to it when he is affected deeply, and personally. On hearing that his favourite son is drowned, Adams falls into a passionate lament. Joseph tries tactfully to remind Adams that he has just been preaching Stoicism and resignation. Just as extreme as his grief, Adams' joy is extravagant when, moments later, he hears that the report was false (IV, viii). In this famous scene, Fielding suggests again that Providence protects the innocent, but Providence does not revive a dead child, nor alter the content of the first message. On the contrary, the false report is a mistake attributable to a human weakness, an eagerness 'from I believe no very good Principle, to relate ill News' (IV, viii). There is no divine interposition; all that is needed to 'save' Adams is to tell him that the first report was false, to disclose the right information. This is not Providence's function, but the author's. By being omniscient and also omnipotent as controller of the fiction, the author is the instrument of Providence for his characters.

One of Fielding's innovations, this narrator who interrupts, digresses, and controls the 'history' is prominent. The narrator continually reminds us that he is the author – unlike Richardson's 'editor' – and discusses his own role, his opinions, and his judgments. Through him, the novel's satiric intentions and its mock-heroic mode of expressing them are accessible to readers who must share his point of view. The narrator sometimes stops for a chat with his reader on a literary or moral subject, or he may remind his reader just what kind of narrative he is reading: in the midst of a mock-heroic description for example:

Reader, we would make a Simile on this Occasion, but for two Reasons: The first is, it would interrupt the Description, which should be *rapid* in this Part; but that doth not weigh much, many Precedents occurring for such an Interruption: The second, and much the greater Reason is, that we could find no Simile adequate for our Purpose: For indeed, what Instance could we bring to set before our Reader's Eyes at once the Idea of Friendship, Courage, Youth, Beauty, Strength, and Swiftness; all which blazed in the Person of *Joseph Andrews*. Let those therefore that describe Lions and Tigers, and Heroes fiercer than both, raise their Poems or Plays with the Simile of *Joseph Andrews*, who is himself above the reach of any Simile. (III, vi)

The technique used here reveals the mechanism of the narrative. Here we see the writer supposedly searching for the right comparison, but, unable to find it, he declares in an interruption that a simile would unfortunately interrupt the description. This statement playfully elevates Joseph to the status of an epic hero, while also drawing attention to the narrator's own function as a go-between and controller of the narrative. Book III, chapter x contains an interlude supposedly designed for no purpose 'but to divert the Reader'. In introducing this chapter, the narrator reminds us of his roles by announcing his interlude and the normal purpose of an interlude in the theatre – 'to entertain you with some excellent Piece of Satire or Humour called a Dance'.

This narrator's plotting has been demonstrably transparent where Adams guesses (wrongly) who Wilson's lost son might be. At a moment when it is clear that the lost child 'had a Mark on his left Breast, of a Strawberry, which his Mother had given him by longing for that Fruit' Adams is declaring that God 'disposes all things for

SHAMELA AND JOSEPH ANDREWS

the best, and very probably he may be some Great Man, or Duke, and may one day or other revisit you in that Capacity' (III, iv). As Adams is thus pointing towards the actions of Providence, Fielding's 'sagacious Reader' recognises that this stock ingredient of a romantic plot has been put there by a narrator who knows more than he is giving away. Again underlining his own role, that narrator also tells us that Wilson will reappear before the end of the novel, 'A Circumstance which we thought too immaterial to mention before' but which will make the reader (for whose welfare the narrator is so solicitous) rejoice at the chance of seeing him again (III, v). All these devices point to a self-conscious narrator who, so far from effacing himself, admits that his ironic panegyric on vanity has been added only to lengthen a short chapter (I, vii), admits with a playful irony that 'As we cannot therefore at present get Mr. *Joseph* out of the Inn, we shall leave him in it, and carry our Reader on after Parson *Adams*' (II, ii), and thus tells us to take note of his own function.

By emphasising this role, Fielding can also emphasise the subjects the narrator discusses, and these in turn lead him to outline his primarily satiric conception of character in this novel. One dominant subject is the nature of the narrative itself, whether it be the division of a book into chapters or the relative merits of biography over romance. In the most important of these disquisitions, the narrator explains his intentions in drawing his characters:

I declare here once for all, I describe not Men, but Manners; not an Individual, but a Species. Perhaps it will be answered, Are not the Characters then taken from Life? To which I answer in the Affirmative; nay, I believe I might aver, that I have writ little more than I have seen. The Lawyer is not only alive, but hath been so these 4000 Years . . . his Appearance . . . is calculated . . . not to expose one pitiful Wretch, to the small and contemptible Circle of his Acquaintance; but to hold the Glass to thousands in their Closets, that they may contemplate their Deformity, and endeavour to reduce it, and thus by suffering private Mortification may avoid public Shame. This places the Boundary between, and distinguishes the Satirist from the Libeller; for the former privately corrects the Fault for the Benefit of the Person, like a Parent; the latter publickly exposes the Person himself, as an Example to others, like an Executioner.   (III, i)

This particular address to the reader establishes that Fielding's presentation of character is satirical (even if his distinction between the satirist and the libeller is less clear than it looks). In all the inns or resting places, 'those little Spaces between our Chapters', as he calls them (II, i), as well as in several fugitive phrases, Fielding speaks of

Joseph Andrews as a biography, itself a species of history. This idea confirms the idea of satiric characterisation.

It was common practice among Fielding's contemporary novelists to pass off novels as 'histories', sometimes as a deliberately misleading disguise, sometimes as a means of lending an air of realism to fiction. *Joseph Andrews* is no exception. The very first sentence of Book I sets out Fielding's understanding of history, as a means of teaching by examples: 'It is a trite but true Observation, that Examples work more forcibly on the Mind than Precepts: And if this be just in what is odious and blameable, it is more strongly so in what is amiable and praise-worthy . . . In this Light I have always regarded those Biographers who have recorded the Actions of great and worthy Persons of both Sexes' (I, i). Fielding's preference for exemplary history places him in a tradition that had been rapidly developed in England during his lifetime. Pope, Swift, and Bolingbroke are the best-known authors to state their belief in the value of exemplary history as a means of promoting virtue and discouraging vice. As we have seen in *Jonathan Wild*, exemplary history was also a vehicle for satire: an example, drawn from history, of a virtuous man, could be used to contrast unfavourably with a living man whom the satirist wished to expose; similarly, an example of a vicious man could provide a parallel with a contemporary villain. A satirist using the 'example' formula would usually claim – with justice – as Fielding does, that he was presenting not an individual, but a species, and thus that the satire transcended topicality by concentrating on the recurrent moral issues of human life and character. Such a definition of exemplary character is at once very different from Richardson's non-satiric conception of his exemplary heroines, Pamela and Clarissa, who never deviate from a stated principle, and are allowed no inconsistency (like Adams') in their temperaments.

We have been introduced to the narrative proper of *Joseph Andrews* with Fielding's statement about examples. If we look back to the preface, we find a wide statement of Fielding's aims:

Now a comic Romance is a comic Epic-Poem in Prose; differing from Comedy, as the serious Epic from Tragedy: its Action being more extended and comprehensive; containing a much larger Circle of Incidents, and introducing a greater Variety of Characters.

The famous phrase, 'a comic Epic-Poem in Prose' has been much debated. It is significant that Fielding speaks of his own work as a 'comic Romance' and that he draws attention to his own extensive use of burlesque and parody, for by these means he allies himself with Cervantes, the author of the greatest comic romance of all; and Fielding also indicates that 'the Classical Reader' will recognise – indeed, look for – the mock-heroic. Any contemporary reader would see in Pope's *Dunciad* an example of a comic-epic poem, and in Fénelon's *Télémaque* an equally well-known example of a prose-epic. But a conflation of the two is an oxymoron (that is, a yoking together of antithetical ideas), and thus Fielding's claim towards the end of the preface is probably ironic:

Having thus distinguished *Joseph Andrews* from the Productions of Romance Writers on the one hand, and Burlesque Writers on the other, and given some few very short Hints (for I intended no more) of this Species of writing, which I have affirmed to be hitherto unattempted in our Language; I shall leave to my good-natur'd Reader to apply my Piece to my Observations, and will detain him no longer than with a Word concerning the Characters in this Work.

Here, Fielding echoes the conventional boast of the epic-poet, that he will, as Milton put it, write 'things unattempted yet in prose or rhyme'. Fielding's irony indicates that *Joseph Andrews* will be a mock-epic, a sure sign of satirical intent, especially after the relatively recent example of *The Dunciad*. The preface to *Joseph Andrews* prepares Fielding's reader for 'a comic Romance', whose dominant aim will be satiric.

It is by no means essential to be familiar with classical epic in order to recognise and appreciate what Fielding is doing in his mock-heroic mode, since the mockery is usually evident through incongruity and exaggeration: it is obvious even when Fielding does not actually tell us that 'the Laws of Heroism' are being violated (II, ix). Fielding expected most of his readers to be reasonably familiar with the classics, but even a nodding acquaintance with just the trappings of heroic literature would be enough to recognise the farcical technique of the novel's most extended – and least subtle – mock-heroic scene, the battle between the travellers and the hounds (III, vi). In this scene, Fielding includes everything: an invocation of the Muse (of biography!), the genealogy of Joseph's cudgel, the intervention of a goddess, and so on. Mock-heroic incongruity consists in the ironic use of such inappropriate descriptive conventions and vocabulary to describe a scuffle between unheroic warriors, who use everyday objects – or, if they are dogs, teeth – for weapons. The description itself begins with two compliments and two jokes (at the expense of Middleton and

Cibber, again) and – ensuring that no one misses the point – ends by directing us to the difference between the language of this specific episode and that of the rest of the novel: 'Thus far the Muse hath with her usual Dignity related this prodigious Battle, a Battle we apprehend never equalled by any Poet, Romance or Life-Writer whatever, and having brought it to a Conclusion she ceased; we shall therefore proceed in our ordinary Style with the Continuation of this History' (III, vi).

This is only one of several examples of Fielding's mock-heroic style. We find a similar tone in passages that mock other forms and styles besides the heroic: for example, the relentless accumulation of examples illustrating surprise (I, viii; II, xiv); the discovery that there has been no sentimental correspondence between Joseph and Fanny, because our heroine is illiterate (I, xi); or the incongruity of describing punches as courtesies and compliments (II,v). The irony that inflates and deflates the participants in a battle, and so sustains these episodes, sustains most of the novel. Fielding's characteristic tone, irony, pervades the descriptions of the characters themselves and their interaction. With an irony that is often far from subtle, Fielding exaggerates his characters while undercutting the very exaggeration of the epic-hero: our heroes are more like mock-heroes or anti-heroes. Unlike the characters who populate an epic-poem, these are ordinary people with ordinary inconsistencies, frailties, and prejudices, yet Fielding allows the conventions of romance to make them heroes. For instance, Fanny Goodwill charms everyone who sets eyes on her – except, of course, the jealous ladies of fashion; Fanny's natural beauty is so dazzling that she is continually a potential victim of the lusts of the ravishers who lurk around every corner. In one of the scenes in which Fanny's chastity is threatened, her assailant finds that Joseph's arrival has brought 'something rougher than the little, tender, trembling Hand of *Fanny*' (IV, vii). Fanny is typically tender, delicate, fearful of real or imagined danger, ready to faint at a moment's notice, and constantly in need of rugged male defence. But *little* she is not. So far from being a beauty of perfect and fashionably slight bodily form, Fanny is a hefty wench with red arms, uneven teeth, a large pockmark, and a ruddy complexion (II, xii). Yet such departures from a conventional, literary excellence are easily, and deliberately, forgotten in the stylised pattern of relationships between her and the two principal characters.

Adams apart, all the characters in the novel tend towards stylisation, even caricature. Since stylisation of character has close affinities with theatrical technique (such as his own, or Ben Jonson's, which Fielding explicitly admires), stylised characters such as Lady Booby, Mrs Slipslop, and Mrs Tow-wouse are sometimes said to represent Fielding's most distinctive mode of characterisation in *Joseph Andrews*. In any case, stylisation and its attendant irony are vital to the satiric function of the characters. A character modelled in part on the fashionable ladies of Restoration comedy, Lady Booby blows hot and cold in her passion for Joseph, yet she expects Slipslop to match her violently changeable moods. Slipslop, often seen as mirroring Lady Booby at a lower social level, is a woman of unbelievable ugliness who, although it is hard to credit, had 'made a small Slip in her Youth' but more plausibly 'had continued a good Maid ever since'. However, she has now 'arrived at an Age when she might indulge herself in any Liberties with a Man, without the danger of bringing a third Person into the World to betray them' (I, vi). Once again, incongruity plays its part, since Slipslop's sexual attractions are so few that her desires are doomed to frustration. But if sexual desire is the motive for most of Slipslop's actions, as it is for most of Lady Booby's, her putting on airs and her habit of using 'hard words' that make her nearly incomprehensible are the defining features of her character. As Maynard Mack has pointed out, there is some truth in the thought that the characters in this novel are recognisable by their idiosyncrasies of speech. Such features make Slipslop unchanging, exaggerated like a caricature, and 'flat', but no less a living character for all that. Much the same is true of the formidably Amazonian innkeeper's wife, Mrs Tow-wouse, also a woman of hideous appearance, whose behaviour is undeviatingly severe, selfish, and unpleasant. From the moment she likens herself to the name on the sign of the inn – the Dragon – we know what to expect of her.

Like Lady Booby, Slipslop, and Mrs Tow-wouse, Beau Didapper embodies an idea rather than a personality; he is a character who, stepping straight from the mildly satiric fictions of the *Tatler*, represents affectation and effeminacy – which do not, however, prevent his attempting to ravish Fanny – so that if we can hardly perceive him as a solid human being, we can at least share the author's ridicule of the Beau's weaknesses. The result of such a satirical conception of character is not so much a knowable individual creature of flesh and blood, but what he appears to represent. Thus, in the same manner as Didapper, Peter Pounce, 'who loved a pretty Girl better than any thing, besides his own Money, or the Money of other People' (III, xii), is evidently the victim of satiric ridicule because of his pathological cupidity, not because he is a recognisable portrait of a living person, although he is that too. The unchanging elements of human nature remain the satirist's targets, and are recognisable as such long after Lord Hervey and Peter Walter have been forgotten as the real originals of Beau Didapper and Peter Pounce.

Joseph Andrews himself falls into this stylised method of characterisation. Joseph's accomplishments are his singing, his strength, and his agility, all of which he puts to good use during the adventures. His attractions (different things to different people) are his good looks and his untrammelled virtue. Unlike Pamela's, Joseph's virtue is not simply his virginity. His virtue consists of his honesty and his unshakeable fidelity to the woman he loves. This virtue expresses itself in chastity, thus in his refusal to forsake Fanny, whatever the temptations. Displaying little real depth of character, Joseph is scarcely more than a representative of innocence and virtue, to such an extent that his protection of his own chastity when Lady Booby lays siege to it, seems ridiculous to us (probably more than it did to Fielding's earliest readers). With all these stylised characters, Fielding makes no attempt to suggest complexity: rather, in the manner of a cartoon, he relies on a few strong lines to indicate one dominant trait. Like caricature, such stylisation suggests moral types rather than rounded individual people, humours rather than complex psyches.

Fielding has been condemned for his willingness to cut a clear distinction between good and evil, or virtue and vice. Hence Adams, Joseph, and Fanny join the former category, Lady Booby, Slipslop, all the ravishers, and most of the innkeepers, the latter. In so far as these characters dramatise conflicts between such opposites, there is justice in the claim. But although stylisation may result in morally simplistic dichotomies, Fielding's characterisation does not create a simple dichotomy between perfect and imperfect people. We have seen how, in a minor way, Fanny is not an impossibly perfect beauty. Similarly, Joseph is not a perfectly formed hero, although we might easily take him for one: as C. J. Rawson has shown, Joseph is in fact more a parody of the elegant, poised gentleman. But these examples may remind us only that this is a tale of low life. In Parson Adams, the real hero of the novel, we find a different kind of imperfection.

Everyone notices how Adams is unable to practise what he preaches. There is an obvious comic disparity between the Stoicism he preaches and his reaction to the news of his little boy's drowning.

There is a similar disparity between his vehement declaration that dispute between two neutral people is pointless and his hurling himself into just such a dispute a few seconds later (II, xi). Fielding adds a further weakness to Adams' temperament:

Indeed if this good Man had an Enthusiasm, or what the Vulgar call a Blind-side, it was this: He thought a Schoolmaster the greatest Character in the World, and himself the greatest of all Schoolmasters, neither of which Points he would have given up to *Alexander the Great* at the Head of an Army.

(III, v)

Even Adams is not entirely free of vanity, neither are his pedagogic achievements quite what he would wish, for his young son proves less competent in Latin than Adams boasts. As if these weaknesses were not enough, Adams is easily duped and believes that his knowledge from reading is superior to that gained by experience. These, certainly, are imperfections in a hero. But in Adams, vanity is a mere blemish and his inability to curb his passions only proof that he is an ordinary man: such weaknesses in other characters usually dominate or define their temperament and action. The major difference between Adams and his opponents is not expressed as a distinction between perfect and imperfect: everyone in this novel is imperfect. The difference is that Adams, Joseph, Fanny, and those who help them are *natural*, but among those whom they encounter, the proud, vain, hypocritical, and evil are unnatural, or artificial.

With his defects, Adams emerges intact from the buffets of the world, for there is nothing defective about his good-natured disposition, his apparently natural love of his fellow men. This quality is what makes Adams the lovable character he is. Without being conventionally or archetypally saintly, Adams is the embodiment of active and practical charity. Charity pours from his heart, as we see when he insists that his wife should share with Joseph and Fanny whatever food and drink there is in the house. Charity is also to be found at the heart of the satire, indeed at the heart of the novel, since charity – above all a social virtue – is missing, for the most part, from the social hierarchy that Fielding portrays.

The mock-heroic technique makes much of social hierarchy. Eighteenth-century Englishmen did a great deal to preserve their hierarchies: conservatives saw in the slightest threat to hierarchical order a threat to stability, prosperity, and peace. Although not an inverted world, the social world of *Joseph Andrews* reveals heroes among the poor and socially low, villains among the wealthy and socially high. One reason why it is difficult to feel much sympathy for Slipslop is that she aspires to a status to which she is not entitled: without being exactly villainous, Slipslop is guilty of vanity, an affectation that belongs to a social class with little to recommend it – since affectation is not natural.

The prevailing social hierarchy, and Adams' place in it, introduces Mrs Slipslop as the parson's sole means of access to the exalted society of the Booby household. Slipslop is the go-between, since these people of fashion consider Adams 'as a kind of Domestic only' (I, iii). Gradually, Slipslop aspires to higher reaches, succeeding only in making herself more ridiculous and odious. This is apparent when she affects not to recognise Fanny, who 'curt'sied, and offered to advance to her; but that high Woman would not return her Curt'sies; but casting her Eyes another way, immediately withdrew into another Room, muttering as she went, she wondered *who the Creature was*' (II, xii). By imitating Lady Booby, Slipslop opens a gap between the heroes and the villains, for she ceases to be a link between them.

The distinction between high and low becomes the subject of the narrator's next chat with his audience, to whom he explains that there is a continuous hierarchy from the lowest servant to the king. He continues:

Nor is there, perhaps, in this whole Ladder of Dependance, any one Step at a greater Distance from the other, than the first from the second: so that to a Philosopher the Question might only seem whether you would chuse to be a great Man at six in the Morning, or at two in the Afternoon. And yet there are scarce two of these, who do not think the least Familiarity with the Persons below them a Condescension, and if they were to go one Step farther, a Degradation. (II, xiii)

The further down that ladder we travel, the more honesty, good-nature, and charity we find. Fielding's anatomy of the social structure exposes the central targets of his satire. These are the people who conceal their true natures, usually according to the dictates of fashion; such people are usually powerful in some way, well-off materially, and given to that affectation mentioned at the start as Fielding's subject. Among the species of people satirised, Fielding numbers the clergy, doctors, innkeepers, justices of the peace, and lawyers.

These characters all adapt their behaviour according to the social status of those they meet, therefore keeping the 'Ladder of Dependance' in existence. Thus innkeepers proportion the quality of their service to the wealth of their guests: to customers with money, they are fulsome, ingratiating, and obsequious; to those of no obvious wealth, they are curt, rude, and imperious. The surgeon likewise

> was more than half drest, apprehending that the Coach had been overturned and some Gentleman or Lady hurt. As soon as the Wench had informed him at his Window, that it was a poor foot Passenger who had been stripped of all he had, and almost murdered; he chid her for disturbing him so early, slipped off his clothes again, and very quietly returned to bed and to sleep.
>   (I, xii)

But once the surgeon takes Joseph for a gentleman (that is, expects a large fee), he exaggerates the seriousness of Joseph's wound. Parson Barnabas neglects his duty, proceeding 'to Prayer with all the expedition he was master of' because he prefers the company and the drink awaiting him in the parlour (I, xiii). Parson Trulliber is interested in Adams only as long as he thinks his visitor has come to buy pigs. With a combination of Slipslop's inflated opinion of herself and *Jonathan Wild*'s inversion of virtue and vice, the lawyer Peter Pounce – far nastier than either Slipslop or Wild – considers Adams too low, and himself too high, to be 'forced to travel about the Country like some People in torn Cassocks, and might be glad to accept of a pitiful Curacy for what I know. Yes, Sir, as shabby Fellows as yourself, whom no Man of my Figure, without that Vice of Good-nature about him, would suffer to ride in a Chariot with him' (III, xiii). But perhaps most disturbing of all is that justices of the peace are not merely ignorant (II, iv; II, xi), but also disposed to judge according to the social status of the accused rather than according to any considerations of the alleged crime. The justices too change their judgments when confronted by a 'gentleman'.

In a social structure like this, life is a struggle for the poor and low, who suffer the insults and indignities forced upon them by the vain and selfish. One of the worst indignities they suffer is made visible to them by the hypocrisy of those whom they ask for help. Attractive as Adams' idealism may be, it is ineffective against the contemptuous ways of the world. Adams expects promises to be kept and actions to match words: unfortunately, life is not like that. A recurrent theme in Fielding's work, the corruption of language plays a part in *Joseph Andrews* as well. There are many examples, from the gibe at Cibber, forced 'against his Inclination . . . to write *English*' (III, vi), to Mrs Slipslop's 'hard Words', from Pounce's dismissal of good nature as a vice to a misunderstanding over the relationship between two 'brother' clergymen. When linguistic corruption betokens hypocrisy, a more serious relationship emerges between word and deed. Barnabas, for instance, has absolutely no idea what Christian forgiveness is, except a form of words (I, xiii), in sharp contrast to Joseph, who does not know either, but does not pretend to know. Similarly, Trulliber is 'reputed a Man of great Charity: for tho' he never gave a Farthing, he had always that Word in his Mouth' (II, xv). The 'natural' of course mean what they say, while the novel's many hypocrites might be willing to talk about helping the poor and needy and suffering, but never to do anything. Hypocrisy in itself is perhaps less important than the uncharitableness to which it points.

In a much quoted episode, a lady of fashion refuses to allow Joseph, beaten up and stripped naked, into the coach beside her. She is accompanied by other passengers who inadvertently display their own hypocrisies, yet – important though the theme of hypocrisy is – it is their total lack of charitable feeling that makes this episode such effective satire. After much altercation, the problem is solved only when the postilion, '(a Lad who hath been since transported for robbing a Hen-roost) had voluntarily stript off a great Coat, his only Garment, at the same time swearing a great Oath, (for which he was rebuked by the Passengers) ''that he would rather ride in his Shirt all his Life, than suffer a Fellow-Creature to lie in so miserable a Condition''' (I, xii). No sooner is that scene concluded than Fielding wades in with more satire of the uncharitable – the surgeon who goes back to bed, and Mrs Tow-wouse's refusal to lend Joseph one of her husband's shirts.

Like the postilion, an anonymous pedlar gives the travellers all the money he has to pay their bill. And Betty, the maid in Mrs Tow-wouse's employ, buys with her own money the tea that Mrs Tow-wouse rudely refuses to give to Joseph. All three of these characters resemble Adams in their impulsive generosity; two of them even give everything they have. Of the three, the only one we get to know at all is Betty. She is another example of a character who is far from perfect: lax in her sexual morals, afflicted by 'a Flame in her, which required the Care of a Surgeon to cool' (I, xviii), and inconstant to her paramour. Yet Betty's character is redeemed, partly by contrast with the frightful Mrs Tow-wouse, partly by her 'Good-nature, Generosity and Compassion' (I, xviii), and partly by contrast with the implied morals of her social superiors. Caught in bed with Mr Tow-wouse, Betty responds violently to the appellation of 'bitch', or rather 'B——':

'I am a Woman as well as yourself,' she roared out, 'and no She-Dog, and
if I have been a little naughty, I am not the first; if I have been no better than
I should be,' cries she sobbing, 'That's no Reason you should call me out of
my Name; my Be—— Betters are wo——worse than me.'   (I, xvii)

Like the postilion's later misdemeanour, mentioned casually in
parenthesis, Betty's sexual promiscuity is unimportant because it is
accompanied by good works; even her sexual favours seem to be
dispensed spontaneously. Yet among Betty's 'betters', the same
unchastity is coupled only with hypocrisy, meanness, and a blunt
refusal to be charitable. Fielding's picture of a social hierarchy
therefore does suggest an inversion of its morality, in that charitable
offices are to be found among those who can least afford them, but
only uncharitableness and unfulfilled promises among those who
could be expected to be generous. If the low are no better than they
should be, socially and individually, the high are worse.

Although, like words, appearances can deceive, actions do not.
These several instances of genuine, active charity are made
prominent by being juxtaposed with contrasting uncharitable
conduct. The 'gentleman', who makes offers and promises that he
cannot and will not fulfil, and whose motives Adams is at a loss to
understand, appears in the middle of a short sequence of examples
which illuminate one another. Before him, the Irish pedlar –
himself contrasting with Trulliber – has given the travellers all his
money; and after the episode of the gentleman's empty promises,
the landlord expresses his trust in Adams, writes off the debt, and
stands the parson another drink. Similarly, when Adams puts all his
money, little though it is, at Joseph's disposal, Fielding points up
the contrast with Mrs Tow-wouse's meanness, for it is only when
money is in evidence that Joseph is 'by Mrs *Tow-wouse's* order
conveyed into a better Bed, and equipped with one of her
Husband's Shirts' (I, xv).

Even the kindness, good nature, and practical generosity of the
Wilson household are contrasted to their opposites. Although the
stories of Wilson and Leonora may appear to be digressive, they are
exemplary tales woven into the thematic and structural unity of the
novel. The two stories offer parallels and contrasts with each other
and with the main narrative. Leonora's want of virtue and her
dedication to selfish ends parallel Wilson's dissipated youth, while
both contrast with the mutual fidelity of Joseph and Fanny. Now in
her retirement, Leonora remains disconsolate, while Wilson lives in
a newly found harmony, from which virtue and charity radiate.
Like these finally differing exemplary tales, each explicit discussion

of charity in the main narrative sets up a contrast between the charitable and the uncharitable, the benevolent and the mean, Parson Adams and the bloodsucking Peter Pounce.

It is because of Methodism's inclination to hypocrisy, to words only, not to actions, that Fielding attacks George Whitefield's doctrine:

'For [asks Adams] can any thing be more derogatory to the Honour of God, than for Men to imagine that the All-wise Being will hereafter say to the Good and Virtuous, Notwithstanding the Purity of thy Life, notwithstanding that constant Rule of Virtue and Goodness in which you walked upon Earth, still as thou did'st not believe every thing in the true Orthodox manner, thy want of Faith shall condemn thee? Or on the other side, can any Doctrine have a more pernicious Influence on Society than a Persuasion, that it will be a good Plea for the Villain at the last day; Lord, it is true I never obeyed one of thy Commandments, yet punish me not, for I believe them all?' 'I suppose, Sir, said the Bookseller, 'your Sermons are of a different Kind.' 'Ay, Sir,' said *Adams*, 'the contrary, I thank Heaven, is inculcated in almost every Page, or I should belye my own Opinion, which hath always been, that a virtuous and good *Turk*, or Heathen, are more acceptable in the sight of their Creator, than a vicious and wicked Christian, tho' his faith was as perfectly Orthodox as St. *Paul's* himself.' (I, xvii)

Adams' opposition to this form of hypocrisy is characteristically uncompromising: he is horrified to think that his sermons might not accurately express his opinion. In that opinion, put into practice by the charitable – Adams, Joseph, Betty, the postilion, one innkeeper, Wilson, the pedlar – *Joseph Andrews* does finally offer a serious moral alternative to the forms of corruption represented by many of the novel's satiric characters. If the novel offers salvation – in the sense that our heroes all attain a happy ending – it is because they practise active virtue and let the consequences be what they may. As M. C. Battestin has shown, Fielding adopted the doctrine known as Latitudinarianism. In this doctrine, virtue is expressed by chastity in the individual, and by charity in society, both of which actions are seen as naturally inherent in man.

Difficult positive values to portray interestingly, chastity and charity are illustrated in *Joseph Andrews* by dramatic and ironic juxtaposition with their opposites. But rather than the parable of innocence and virtue that some see, *Joseph Andrews* is a comic novel underpinned by these moral themes. Fielding is not quite even-handed in his treatment of these two related species of virtue: he is harder on the uncharitable than he is on the unchaste. For although he might laugh with good humour at the attempted unchastity of

Lady Booby and Mrs Slipslop, he also scorns them for their lack of charity. Yet Fielding treats Betty the maid, herself far from chaste, with nothing like scorn: despite a superficial similarity, these women are profoundly different when it comes to the social virtue of charity, for then Betty is open and generous, the other two insincere and therefore contemptible. Still, while this does not mean that Fielding unconditionally condones unchastity, he was – until he created Amelia – too much of a realist to think that paragons of virtue actually exist. In Fielding's comic and satiric vision, anyone who disguises his or her inner nature is essentially dishonest and is therefore fit only to be laughed at.

Most modern readers probably think of *Joseph Andrews* as a novel, but by comparison with the novels of Henry James or James Joyce, it is bound to seem very unsophisticated. Fielding himself, however, did not see *Joseph Andrews* as a novel, but as a romance. In 1780 Thomas Holcroft conveniently expressed what had become a standard formal distinction when he demanded of the novel a unity of design, and thus exclusion of incidents irrelevant to the story. As the eighteenth century slowly came to accept its novels as literature, the demand grew for realism, to which romance could not aspire. Certainly, *Joseph Andrews* inverts many of the standard features of romance, as William Congreve famously defined them in the preface of his own *Incognita: A Novel* (1692),

Romances are generally composed of the Constant Loves and invincible Courages of Hero's, Heroins, Kings and Queens, Mortals of the first Rank, and so forth; where lofty Language, miraculous Contingencies and impossible Performances, elevate and surprize the Reader into a giddy Delight . . . he is forced to be very well convinced that 'tis all a lye. Novels are of a more familiar nature; Come near us, and represent to us Intrigues in practice, delight us with Accidents and odd Events, but not such as are wholly unusual or unpresidented, . . . Romances give more of Wonder, Novels more Delight. (Preface)

'History' can be explained in several ways. Not only was it a usefully misleading label, it was also a term used to describe medieval romances as well as biographies. Despite Fielding's claim that *Joseph Andrews* is a biography, we learn actually very little about Joseph, whose 'history' is almost incidental. But there is much in *Joseph Andrews* reminiscent of medieval romance: for instance, the moral fable, the many caricatures, the allegorical structure of events. Joseph is something like a parody of the brave knight who rescues a damsel in distress and conducts her safely home, and so forth.

Joseph Warton reported in 1746 that Fielding valued *Joseph Andrews* 'above all his writings': this was before *Tom Jones*. If we think of the most widely read of all the early novelists, Defoe, Richardson, and Fielding, we find that they are not only profoundly different from later novelists, but also markedly different from one another. Defoe's technique is unashamedly picaresque and seemingly haphazard in structure; Richardson carefully presents correspondence between characters; Fielding constantly interrupts the narrative and delights in his own artifice. All of these writers created fiction that was supposed to reflect reality in some degree – in a way that romance really never does. Of the three, Fielding makes the smallest effort to disguise his fiction as reality itself. A narrator who interrupts his narrative to tell us what will happen to his characters has clearly resigned any claim on our credulity. Unlike Defoe and Richardson, Fielding keeps us consciously distanced from his characters, however much we may recognise them as 'real' human beings. By glorying in his own artifice (a technique learned in journalism) Fielding can glorify art as an ordered, shaped, satisfying construct. The coincidences in his plot, the saving hand of Providence, the nick-of-time escapes: these suggest something far removed from realism, something more like an exemplary moral tale, presided over by an artist who resembles a providential deity. Certainly, at this point in his career, Fielding seems to have been most concerned with the moral issues: to confront them is to confront major issues in everyday life. The subject, therefore, is appropriate for realism, but the treatment is not.

4

Tom Jones

After the *Miscellanies* and *Joseph Andrews*, Fielding had work to do. He was an active barrister on the western circuit until October 1748, when he took up new duties as a magistrate for the city of Westminster. Soon afterwards he was able to combine this with a magistracy for the county of Middlesex. Fielding had also been writing: in the five years up to 1748 he produced two prefaces and five underrated fictional letters for his sister Sarah's books, seven political pamphlets, one journalistic pamphlet, and a 'paraphrase' of the first book of Ovid's *Ars Amatoria*. Overshadowing this output in quantity were two newspapers he ran almost single-handed: the *True Patriot*, which existed for thirty-two issues from 5 November 1745 to 17 June 1746 (and two more were issued later), and the *Jacobite's Journal*, forty-nine issues from 5 December 1747 to 5 November 1748. Neither of these periodicals has the charm or vitality of the *Champion*, but they both have their moments.

In the middle of this activity, the 1745 Jacobite rebellion took place. The first issue of the *True Patriot* appeared as the romantic rebel hero, Bonnie Prince Charlie, was about to storm Carlisle. A month later he heeded his counsellors' advice to retreat north from the midlands. Despite occasional military successes, the Jacobite army was on the defensive if not on the run during the winter. Their famous rout came at Culloden in April 1746. The rest of that year brought trials, executions, and the transportation of convicted Jacobites. The *True Patriot* offers commentary on the politics of the rebellion and its aftermath. Fielding had previously voiced political judgments (mostly in satire) that aligned him with the 'country' opposition, until around 1742 a miscellaneous coalition of Whigs and Tories, Hanoverians and Jacobites. Fielding's politics were anti-Walpole at times, but in common with so many of Walpole's opponents, Fielding was opposed mainly to Walpole's cynical system of government based on corruption. The story of Fielding's politics is difficult and complicated, because his loyalties seem to have shifted more than once. There is, however, no doubt about one thing: although he satirised the Hanoverians in his *Natural History of the Hanover Rat* (1744), he supported the Hanoverian establishment,

73

as his two periodicals in this decade testify. The arguments, fictions, squibs, lampoons, and satires – in fact, the whole editorial slant of the *True Patriot* – are unequivocally anti-Jacobite. The *Jacobite's Journal* is a different kind of paper, less committed to dynastic politics than its title implies. This paper is conducted by 'John Trott-Plaid, Esq.' an ironically committed Jacobite who actually discusses other, more pressing affairs than the dead Stuart cause. In the winter of 1747–8 it was more important to end British involvement in the War of the Austrian Succession. A peace treaty was signed at Aix-la-Chapelle in October 1748 to put an end to the war. Two months later, now installed as a London magistrate, Fielding finished with the *Jacobite's Journal* and, two months after that, in early February 1749, *Tom Jones* was at last published. The new novel was printed in six volumes, at the fairly expensive price of eighteen shillings.

News leaked out that Fielding was writing a substantial novel. During 1748 there was excited expectation, because while Fielding was at work, Richardson was beginning to publish another improbably lengthy set of fictional correspondence: *Clarissa*. Richardson's seven volumes appeared at intervals between December 1747 and December 1748. Fielding had detested *Pamela*, but he was generous in his praise of *Clarissa*, even to the extent of writing to Richardson to explain why he found one scene particularly moving. Richardson did not return the compliment: as far as we know, he refused even to read *Tom Jones*. In 1752, exulting over the mixed reception of Fielding's *Amelia*, Richardson dismissed the 'vogue' for Fielding occasioned by 'the success his spurious brat Tom Jones so unaccountably met with' (*Correspondence, III*, 33–4). The warm, humane Fielding contrasts with the cold, envious Richardson. Their new novels both appealed to the reading public. Sales figures for *Clarissa* have not survived, but we know that it sold quite well, though not well enough to satisfy Richardson completely. With a sale of 10,000 in nine months, *Tom Jones* perhaps had the edge. Reprints and new editions of both novels were called for in London, while translations were quickly under way in Germany and France. By the end of the century, both were available in six European languages besides English and both had been adapted for the stage.

Exactly when Fielding wrote *Tom Jones* is not certain. The closing chapters show signs of great haste, with Fielding rushing to his conclusion and sometimes forgetting what he has written: he was therefore almost certainly still writing as late as the last months of 1748. In the absence of much hard evidence, Martin C. Battestin has argued, entirely plausibly, that some parts of the novel were composed in the early summer of 1745, when the Jacobite rising was in the air. Using the events of 1745, the middle third of the novel cleverly intertwines fictional and contemporary political history. There, Tom Jones decides to volunteer for the army against the rebels, and a part of his journey coincides with that of troops in the west of England in 1745. Political character is prominent in *Tom Jones*: aside from Jones himself, Partridge is a secret Jacobite sympathiser, and Squire Western a dyed-in-the-wool Jacobite, though his politics are based on ignorance and half-ignorant assumptions, not on any coherent principle or policy. But Jacobite myth runs much more deeply in *Tom Jones*, as Ronald Paulson has recently pointed out. Tom Jones himself may be a reminder of the gallant, romantic prince.

The middle third of the novel, particularly, mingles fictional and real history. In a parallel way, the whole novel mingles fictional and real places and people. Inns are identified, and so are some of the innkeepers. The mixture of mythologising, fiction, and reality is unlikely to delude many readers into thinking of all the people, places, and events of *Tom Jones* as having an independent existence outside the pages of the novel. But the mixture creates a strong sense of *Tom Jones* as an imagined paradigm of the real world. The novel is not, finally, realistic, but exemplary.

Fielding does not pretend that *Tom Jones* is anything but fiction. Similarly, with *Clarissa* Richardson stops pretending that he is the editor of genuine correspondence. But Richardson did not make any claim to be the author. He intended *Clarissa* to be, if anything, more exemplary than *Tom Jones* turned out to be. *Tom Jones* was not a response to *Clarissa*. Although Fielding occasionally alludes to *Clarissa*, sometimes even inviting comparison, he did not encourage any rivalry between himself and Richardson. Nevertheless, literary history has characterised them as rivals.

Because of the dominance of these two novels, it has become almost customary to view the mid-eighteenth-century novel as virtually the property of only Fielding and Richardson. This does a disservice to Smollett, especially, but also to a host of more minor and now often forgotten novelists – particularly women – who developed and explored established forms of narrative fiction. The varied achievement of these minor authors was important for the emergence of the novel, but Fielding shows almost no sign of response to this body of writing at all. There is no evidence in *Tom Jones* or anywhere else that Fielding had even read such novelists as

Defoe, Eliza Haywood, Penelope Aubin, Mary Davys, or William Chetwood. Fielding was clearly not alone in writing novels, yet he probably did more – alone – than any other writer to improve the literary status of the novel at mid-century.

Contemporaries compared Fielding and Richardson at once. At first Richardson was seen as a sentimental but profound moralist, Fielding as realistic but immoral. A little over two centuries later, both writers had been radically revalued, with an almost exact reversal of these estimates. Now that Fielding has many devoted admirers to vouch for his seriousness, Richardson is just beginning to be seen once more by professional critics as perhaps the more important. But Fielding, I think, is still the more widely read.

Dr Johnson recommended reading *Clarissa* not for its story but for its sentiment. This seems fair enough, but his famous words to Hannah More, that he was 'shocked' to hear her 'quote from so vicious a book' as *Tom Jones*, sound rather quaint now. No one now is very likely to think of this novel as 'corrupt' or 'vicious'. Still, as John Osborne's 1963 film script demonstrates, *Tom Jones* may yet be regarded in some quarters as little more than a jolly, sexual romp through 'Merrie England'. There is no reason why a film should follow a novel at all closely, or indeed at all, but if Osborne's script is taken to be a direct interpretation of Fielding's novel, *Tom Jones* emerges as a rather shallow series of harmless escapades, albeit touched with satire. But Fielding's novel is not like this. It is funny, witty, and entertaining, and it does contain a series of sexual escapades, in bushes, bedrooms, and boudoirs. However, it is also a serious, moralistic novel, ingeniously constructed around coincidences so implausible in their number and kind as to deny realistic intent.

So perhaps the first question one might ask is: what kind of book is *Tom Jones*? Fielding called it history: *The History of Tom Jones, A Foundling*. Provoking, teasing, and stimulating his readers throughout this long narrative, Fielding continually draws attention to the kind of book he is writing. He reminds us seven more times that it is history, but he also claims, in a famous phrase, to be 'the Founder of a new Province of Writing' whose laws he is at liberty to make up. He therefore warns us of his own caprice as a narrator, while also telling us to expect something different. Elsewhere he speaks of his work as 'Comedy' and as belonging to 'that Kind of Novels, which . . . is of the comic Class' (XIV. i). To add to a confusion of which Tristram Shandy would be proud, Fielding likens his novel to a stage ('the theatre of this history') on which his characters perform, while we the audience respond in accordance with the social status of the seats we occupy in the theatre of the world. As if that were not enough, he lays down 'Rules' for 'Prosai-comi-epic Writing' (V. i). This last, in fact, is our most graspable but least helpful clue, for *Tom Jones*, rather than *Joseph Andrews*, seems closer to being Fielding's comic epic-poem in prose, now called an 'Heroic, Historical, Prosaic Poem' (IV. i). In addition, it has been a critical commonplace, despite articulate opposition, that *Tom Jones* was Fielding's 'real' comic-epic. I mentioned in connection with *Tom Thumb* the eighteenth century's high esteem for epic and tragedy, and its failure to write worthwhile examples of either. As long as Homer was a model, it seems, epic-poems were translatable but not imitable. Epic-poetry, as Pope for instance recognised, was a form of history: it was a chronicle of heroic and glorious times, and therefore often tended to be unashamedly patriotic. Lord Bolingbroke, disinclined as usual to idealise, thought Homer had written the *Iliad* only because he 'meant to flatter his countrymen, by recording the feats of his ancestors'. Some critics argue that the evolving novel simply replaces these older forms, others that history – such as Gibbon's *Decline and Fall of the Roman Empire* – was a substitute for epic. Others still argue that *Tom Jones* is a surrogate epic, *Clarissa* a surrogate tragedy. However, these are our terms, not Fielding's. 'Epic' in the mid-eighteenth century did not have the range of connotations it has for us today. We should remember that to Fielding – himself hardly a theorist – 'epic' would mean little more than 'long narrative'.

'History' also meant 'narrative', of course. But 'history' was used on title-pages of fictitious biographies and medieval romances. The stubborn idea that *Tom Jones* is a comic-epic is in fact based on an unhistorical assumption. In places Fielding indulges in mock-epic, but almost nowhere in classical epic imitation. An epic, for one thing, would start *in medias res*, and would consist, typically, of a series of narratives of past glories, all well known to the listeners. But the 'historical arrangement' of *Tom Jones* chronicles the life of the hero from his obscure birth to his happy marriage: this structure is characteristic of romance, not epic.

Fielding's jokey phrase, 'comic Epic-Poem in Prose', is a slight foundation for a novelist's alleged theory. Where it occurs in the preface to his previous romance, *Joseph Andrews*, the expression may half-conceal an attempt to write an epic while all around are struggling but failing to write theirs. However, it is more likely that, by associating his work with epic – however obliquely – Fielding was making some small claim for the literary seriousness of the 'new': the 'novel'. Where he does seem to be imitating the epic, his claim in *Tom Jones* that he has founded 'a new Province of Writing' (II. i) is a distant echo of the epic-poet's entirely conventional boast that he writes things no one has written before. Near the middle of *Tom Jones* he reinforces this claim by introducing a 'Description hitherto unessayed in Prose or Verse' (IX. v), the traditional boast now applied to just a short passage. The concomitant part of Fielding's claim to originality is that he is 'at liberty to make what Laws I please' (V. i). This is a paradoxical and poker-faced parody of a famous critical dictum. The French critic René le Bossu had defended the 'right' of the ancients not to have their 'rules' disregarded by upstart moderns. Fielding claims to be a modern not bound by ancient rules because he is not writing in an ancient form. But although several of Fielding's critical pronouncements in *Tom Jones* claim to be original, in truth they are classical axioms.

The literary models to which Fielding looks are old, established by tradition, and yet, as Ian Watt has argued, since Homer's comic-epic never survived, neither Fielding nor anyone else could have any idea what a classical comic-epic was like. An analogy between his own fiction and the lost *Margites* could therefore not be taken very far. One reason why, in *Tom Jones*, Fielding imitates only loosely some of the characteristics of known classical epics, is simply that he had no heroic deeds at his disposal, no ready-made history to exploit patriotically, unless it were to be the suppression of the Jacobite rebellion. Therefore, fundamentally, *Tom Jones* lacks the seriousness of the heroic and has little chance of imitating a lost comic-epic. Although Fielding does imitate classical epics very occasionally, he does not actually purport to be following in the tradition of the classical epic-poets. Instead, when he celebrates his literary models, the company he says he keeps is not Homer or Virgil, but this list of comic writers inspired by the Spirit of Genius, whom he invokes:

Come thou, that hast inspired thy *Aristophanes*, thy *Lucian*, thy *Cervantes*, thy *Rabelais*, thy *Molière*, thy *Shakespeare*, thy *Swift*, thy *Marivaux*, fill my Pages with Humour; till Mankind learn the Good-Nature to laugh only at the Follies of others, and the Humility to grieve at their own.   (XIII. i)

Thus armed with the traditions of comedy, satire, and romance, Fielding can pretend to give the eighteenth century the epic its writers might have been hoping to contrive, yet he actually writes a comic-satiric romance.

It may be surprising that so many critics persist in calling *Tom Jones* an epic. But in some respects it is legitimate to do so, if only loosely. For although *Tom Jones* imitates classical epic in only the most casual and incidental ways, the novel has a kind of moral heroism reminiscent of Virgil or even Spenser, and an explicit tendency to universality. Fielding promises (when he says he may make his own laws) a large, sweeping treatment of time, which helps to create distance and perspective. These features all connote the large scale that 'epic' signifies to us in modern everyday use.

Fielding says he intends to leave out great tracts of time when nothing important happened, and to record only the history of 'those notable Æras when the greatest Scenes have been transacted on the human Stage' (II. i). Statements with such generalising implications are scattered everywhere in *Tom Jones*. They contribute perhaps more than anything else to the sense that this novel is about the human race, not the individual but the species. Generality is also conveyed by Fielding's love of abstracts and generalisations. He often generalises an incident or a relationship. An account of the friction between Captain Blifil and Bridget Allworthy leads to a discussion of 'the married State'. A comment on Sophia's perfect good-breeding leads to a generalisation about 'Ease' in one's behaviour in 'what is called the polite Circle'. By this means Fielding's appeal is often directed to his reader's knowledge and experience of the world, to a generality that is exemplified by the particular incidents of Fielding's own story. Particular incidents therefore often acquire the nature of examples of human conduct, as if the whole novel were a kind of casebook. Added to this, a large and varied cast of characters populates what seems to be a wide world, as in *Joseph Andrews*, so that variety can suggest inclusiveness. In *Joseph Andrews* Fielding speaks of *Don Quixote* as 'a History of the World in general'; the phrase can be equally well applied to Fielding's own intentions in *Tom Jones*. It makes more sense to look at *Tom Jones* as a panoramic novel, because its daring breadth is far more effectively functional than Fielding's few scattered – and confusing – remarks about epic writing.

With his readers primed to expect the highlights of history, and a variety of characters, in the first third of the novel Fielding introduces some twenty characters and speeds through twenty years. Some modern critics see the remainder of the novel as Tom Jones' journey through life, to maturity and wisdom. Truly, the novel does give us such a sense of expansiveness, in time and space, but Jones' journey actually occupies only forty-two days, into which time an incredible wealth of experience is crammed. Fielding's selective treatment of time is therefore obviously not naturalistic, and neither is his treatment of character. Both time and character create generality.

As before, Fielding's customary stylisation of his characters makes them exemplary, and thus to some extent generalised. He had not changed this primarily satiric conception of character. Although *Tom Jones* is not a satiric novel, it contains many of Fielding's typical satiric subjects and stances. Servants can always be relied upon to respond to the lure of gold; with profit in mind, innkeepers adjust their behaviour according to the status (actual or assumed) of their customers; surgeons exaggerate the seriousness of minor wounds; lawyers dispute incomprehensibly. Avarice and ambition, ingratitude and uncharitableness, recur in *Tom Jones*. Fielding also uses the same satiric techniques as before: the ironic commentary most of all, but also the contrast between what people say and do. For example, with a combination of these favourite techniques, he reveals the motive behind Captain Blifil's desire to marry Bridget Allworthy:

> To deal plainly with the Reader, the Captain, ever since his arrival, at least from the Moment his Brother had proposed the Match to him, long before he had discovered any flattering Symptoms in Miss *Bridget*, had been greatly enamoured; that is to say, of Mr. *Allworthy*'s House and Gardens, and of his Lands, Tenements and Hereditaments; of all which the Captain was so passionately fond, that he would most probably have contracted Marriage with them, had he been obliged to have taken the Witch of *Endor* into the Bargain.
> (I. xi)

Because he thinks Allworthy might disapprove, the Captain 'resolved to take all private Opportunities of making his Addresses; but in the Presence of Mr. *Allworthy* to be as reserved, and as much upon his Guard as was possible' (I. xi). The final satiric deflation of the misguided Captain (who has entirely misjudged Allworthy) is also a splendid piece of Fielding's casual, ironic comedy. Captain Blifil meditates his 'intended Alterations in the House and Gardens' and many other schemes involving his spending of Allworthy's money:

> Nothing was wanting to enable him to enter upon the immediate Execution of this Plan, but the Death of Mr. *Allworthy* . . .
> But while the captain was one Day busied in deep Contemplation of this Kind, one of the most unlucky, as well as unseasonable Accidents,

happened to him. The utmost Malice of Fortune could indeed have contrived nothing so cruel, so mal-a-propos, so absolutely destructive to all his Schemes. In short, not to keep the Reader long in Suspense, just at the very Instant when his Heart was exulting in Meditations on the Happiness which would accrue to him by Mr. *Allworthy*'s Death, he himself – died of an Apoplexy. (II. viii)

This is classic satire that diminishes its subject by ridicule. Captain Blifil's avarice is no less odious for being risible; he is also uncharmingly ruthless. But if the Captain's self-interest is unamiable, his son's is far more unattractive. Blifil junior is so thoroughly evil that he is too dangerous to be laughed at. His machinations might resemble his father's, or Jonathan Wild's for that matter, but Blifil is not ridiculed like these other characters. He is just as much a satiric example as Pope's amalgam of evil, Sporus (in the *Epistle to Dr Arbuthnot*).

Satiric examples like these characters often imply generality. It has been argued, too, that Tom Jones represents a large number of his countrymen, or even that he is an Everyman figure, because he bears two of the commonest names in England. The other most important character, Sophia, has some obvious symbolic significance, too, since her name means 'wisdom'. Allworthy is generally recognised to be a fictional equivalent of the great philanthropist, Ralph Allen, who is complimented several times in *Tom Jones* and elsewhere in Fielding's writing. But while Allen – or possibly Lyttelton, to whom *Tom Jones* is dedicated – may lie behind Allworthy, the character is not a specific representation of any real man.[1] His name suggests not that he is too good to be true, but that his moral conduct is unimpeachable because his heart is always in the right place. However, neither Allen nor anyone else could be flattered by a portrait of one so gullible, so naive that Blifil imposes upon him with almost contemptuous ease. Allworthy's is another name suggestive of the morality play, or of the 'humour' type of character of Fielding's own drama. Plausible or not, Allworthy is a type, and types offer us generality rather than individuality.

[1] Ralph Allen (1693–1764) was famous for his reform of the cross-country postal system, his charity, and his hospitality at his mansion near Bath, Prior Park. He was also known for his patronage of literature and friendship with many writers, including Fielding, his sister Sarah, Richardson, and Pope. George Lyttelton (1709–73) was an old friend of Fielding's who was similarly well known for his benevolence and his friendship with Pope. A member of the opposition to Walpole in the 1730s, Lyttelton was a lord of the Treasury in the new government – the so-called Broad-Bottom Administration – led by Henry Pelham from December 1744.

There are, of course, exceptions: characters who seem to have more individuality than generality, such as Thwackum, Square, Western, Aunt Western. Their names, too, have some mild significance at the level of humours (but does Bridget Allworthy?). As often in Fielding's fiction, some of his best comic creations are these secondary characters. They have both the vividness of caricature and its individuality, but also its limitations. Thus although these characters have perhaps more individuality, more specificity, than Jones or Sophia, they are always extremely simple, more recognisable and predictable. In the cases of Thwackum and Square, Fielding even hints that they too are satiric types: 'Had not *Thwackum* too much neglected Virtue, and *Square* Religion, in the Composition of their several Systems; and had not both utterly discarded all natural Goodness of Heart, they had never been represented as the Objects of Derision in this History' (III. iv). Western's definite presence brings life and colour to the narrative, as well as affording Fielding an opportunity for good humour, yet Western remains only a variation on a stock theme. He is quite an amiable buffoon until he becomes a tyrant at the first sign of resistance to his will. He is also sentimental; if he loses his temper quickly, he regains it (with a tear of joy) equally quickly. But he is the archetypal boorish Jacobite country squire, devoted to hunting, drinking, and the uncomplicated country life. Even Western must be able to command a reader's sympathy: the happy outcome at the end depends in part on his restored affability. Although his great affection for Tom is transformed in an instant to homicidal intent, so too must his fury be assuaged in a matter of seconds.

As a feminist political commentator, Aunt Western is unusually in advance of her time, but she is developed no further. In hers and all these cases, it would be easy to give each character a label consisting of a short defining phrase: Square the deist who is virtuous only in theory (III. iii),[1] Thwackum the fierce defender of orthodoxy (and physical violence – at least to one pupil), and so forth. Taken together, all the characters create the variety that generates the sense of an inclusive and expansive world. In creating universality, Fielding pays a price. *Tom Jones* has no rival to Parson Adams (who is briefly mentioned at the end). One of the finest of Fielding's vital comic characters, Adams is the exception to the stylisation of characters in *Joseph Andrews*. In *Tom Jones*, the

---

[1] A deist was generally someone who believed that God had nothing to do with the laws of the universe after the Creation. Because deists denied divine revelation, they were often considered in the eighteenth century to be atheists.

characters are if anything more stylised still, their action and interaction more deliberately balanced and controlled. However eccentric Adams is, he brings human warmth and a touch of realism to *Joseph Andrews*.

Neither Partridge, nor Allworthy, nor Jones, can rival Adams. Partridge is eccentric, superstitious, and garrulous, but he lacks Adams' good nature and barely rises above the level of caricature. With the really lifeless figure of Allworthy, Fielding comes close to the technique of sentimental characterisation, by not telling us what Allworthy looks like, but telling us almost *ad nauseam* how good he is. Only Jones might approach the status of Adams, but for all his vivacity, his admirable honour, and his good nature, Jones does not have that charming, impulsive simplicity that wins our affection for Adams.

The virtuous characters are fairly freely adapted from the sentimental tradition, to recommend virtue. But while tears flow in decently sentimental quantities, virtue in *Tom Jones* is not embodied in slightly ridiculous characters like Joseph Andrews, nor in mostly passive victims like the Heartfrees. Virtue is an active principle: it is good nature in practice. It is noticeable that Parson Adams is well-built, strong, a good fighter. So too is Tom Jones: he is physically active, tough, and athletic. For one thing, Jones contrasts conspicuously with the truly repulsive Blifil, whose repressed sexuality eventually expresses itself as the tortured lust of a potential rapist (VII. vi). Jones' virtue is associated with his vigour, robustness, and a general sense of health. Blifil's vice, on the contrary, goes well with his physical nastiness. Sophia, who finds Blifil repellent, is herself very far from passive: like Fanny she might be a potential victim of male lust, but she is resourceful and determined, as well as good-natured.

Although many of the characters in *Tom Jones* are marvellously entertaining, they are not especially varied in themselves, nor really particularly interesting as people, but rather representatives or examples of moral traits and temperaments. This accords with Fielding's much-discussed principle of 'Conservation of Character', which he significantly attributes to 'dramatic Critics' (actually Aristotle and Horace). This principle demands that actions should be plausibly human and that 'they should be likely for the very Actors and Characters themselves to have performed' (VIII. i). Each character is thus self-consistent, but not necessarily complex. Fielding has his characters play out a complex game, whose patterns of movement are more important than the pieces he moves. As Battestin has shown, Jones' progress from the west country to London serves to underscore his parallel progress through error, indiscretion, and misjudgment, to worldly wisdom. That progress, on both levels, is the centre of an ingenious structure of events. It is to this quite startlingly complex structure that I shall now turn.

The structure of *Tom Jones* has always been an object of wonder. In the first edition, Fielding divided his narrative into six volumes, three books to a volume: the first six books describe life at Paradise Hall; the middle six, events on the road; the last six, events in London. In a remarkable essay, Frederick W. Hilles likens this tripartite structure of the narrative to the characteristic ground plan of a Palladian country house – in particular that of Prior Park, Ralph Allen's mansion at Bath. Fielding speaks of Prior Park by name in *Tom Jones*, incorporates some parts of the estate in his description of Paradise Hall, and compliments Allen. It is also likely that some parts of the novel were written during some of Fielding's many visits as Allen's guest at Prior Park. Hilles was the first critic to speak convincingly of the 'architecture' of *Tom Jones*, in which every part has a counterpart, and an almost mathematical exactness disposes incidents in parallel and characters in contrasts. The novel is certainly arranged with an ingenuity which, to borrow a line from Pope, ensures that 'Parts answ'ring parts shall slide into a whole'. The importance of this elegant, proportioned structure can hardly be overestimated.

In determining the relation of the parts to the whole, Fielding was convinced that a sequence of little incidents and circumstances rapidly grew large:

> In reality, there are many little Circumstances too often omitted by injudicious Historians, from which Events of the utmost Importance arise. The World may indeed be considered as a vast Machine, in which the great Wheels are originally set in Motion by those which are very minute, and almost imperceptible to any but the strongest Eyes. (V. iv)

Fielding's own complicated plot makes use of so many apparent trifles linked together to form his great machine. In all, every detail will have its part to play in the total design: Sophia's muff (V. iv), the lawyer Dowling's great haste, and the explanation of what passed between him and Blifil (V. vii; VIII. viii; XII. ix; XII. x; XIII. v; and XVIII. viii), Black George's theft of Jones' £500 bill, and its subsequent turning up (VI. xiii; XVIII. viii). All these function as catalysts. They are as important in their way as

Desdemona's handkerchief. The plot hurries to its final resolution with a deathbed revelation, concealed letters, and no time for anything else, 'as we have now Leisure only to what is very material' (XVIII. x).

In a lengthy explanation Fielding warns his reader 'not too hastily to condemn any of the Incidents in this our History, as impertinent and foreign to our main Design, because thou dost not immediately conceive in what Manner such Incident may conduce to that Design. This Work may, indeed, be considered as a great Creation of our own' (X. i). With signposts like this before our eyes, we cannot fail to recognise Fielding's intentions. Every apparent digression is relevant to the main design. When Jones sees 'his good Offices to [Mrs Miller] and her Family brought to a happy Conclusion' (XV. viii), the narrator concludes:

Those Readers who are of the same Complexion with him will perhaps think this short Chapter contains abundance of Matter; while others may probably wish, short as it is, that it had been totally spared as impertinent to the main Design, which I suppose they conclude is to bring Mr. *Jones* to the Gallows, or if possible, to a more deplorable Catastrophe.   (XV. viii)

The importance of the chapter therefore lies not in Nightingale's marriage to Nancy, but in Jones' generous behaviour: that is what belongs to the main design, for the main design is concerned with moral conduct. In the best discussion of the novel's structure, Martin Battestin declares that 'Design is the matrix of plot in *Tom Jones*; it is the primary (if not the only) determining factor in the structure of the book' (*Providence of Wit*, p. 148). The whole point about design is that it presupposes a designer.

Fielding explicitly imitates the philosophy of the design argument (as it is, and was, known). This is the venerable theory that nature reveals to us evidence of pattern, organisation, and structure, everywhere from the smallest insect to the planetary system. This (the theory argues) must have been created deliberately, because chance or accident could never be responsible for such order. Therefore a designer created nature: that is, God exists. Two other variations of the design argument show God as supreme architect and supreme artist. Recently, the design argument had been given new impetus and a new emphasis by a number of microscopists, and by Sir Isaac Newton, better known in his own day as a theologian than as a mathematician. Newton's scientific discoveries persuaded him that God was a geometrician and a mechanic. Fielding's ow imitation of the design argument places the author in the same relation to his writing as God to His universe. This is a commonplace with a very long history. The inclusive design of *Tom Jones* thus seems to be an affirmation that Design determines the nature of the world: a Christian vision of life itself. But Fielding's facetiousness and irony, his lightness of tone, his uppishness when he addresses his readers: all these tend to undermine the apparently serious proposition that he is an analogue of God. *Tom Jones* is enjoyed by so many readers not because it is a solemn affirmation of Christian values, but because it is a good-humoured, relaxed, funny affirmation that the good are rewarded in the fictional world. The design of the novel also satisfies anyone's desire for completed, ordered, balanced things.

Very little in this narrative is left unexplained. In Book I, any reader knows on a first reading that the foundling's true parentage will be revealed in due course. Since Jenny Jones knows who the mother is, but refuses to say, it is obvious that she will have some later part to play in the expected revelation. But Fielding has to remind us, in a subordinate clause, that 'it will be some Time before [the reader] will hear any more of *Jenny*' (I. ix). When she does reappear, with her name conveniently changed so that we do not know who she is, the only person in the inn at Upton who could recognise and identify her is Partridge, her former employer. But Fielding naturally and inconspicuously keeps him from seeing her. This occurs near the middle of the novel (IX. vi), but not until near the end are we triumphantly told that this was all part of the author's brilliant scheme:

If the Reader will please refresh his Memory, by turning to the Scene at *Upton* in the Ninth Book, he will be apt to admire the many strange Accidents which unfortunately prevented any Interview between *Partridge* and Mrs. *Waters*, when she spent a whole Day there with Mr. *Jones*. Instances of this Kind we may frequently observe in Life, where the greatest Events are produced by a nice Train of little Circumstances; and more than one Example of this may be discovered by the accurate Eye, in this our History.   (XVIII. ii)

While this imitates the 'vast Machine' theory of the world, such a self-conscious artifice gives shape to the plot, whereas in most contemporary novels, chance or fortune is more likely to dictate the pattern of events. Fielding refuses to pretend that fortune is so responsible, for he knows that authors create fictional fortune. This is art, not life.

Fielding's didactic artifice draws our attention to what we are allowed to know and what we must know. His artifice also gives him a chance to investigate motives by making them integral to his palpably contrived plot. Writing letters while locked in her room, Clarissa and her correspondents can usually reveal only their own motives. Moll Flanders can only guess – if she is interested – at the motives of other people she meets. Where Richardson and Defoe necessarily restrict their narrative opportunities, Fielding's plot, as well as his omniscient narrator, need not impose any such restrictions. Because nothing is (apparently) ever the result of chance, but everything caused by deliberate contrivance, Fielding has the opportunity to explore the motive behind every human action – since every action in his plot is a part of his total, overall design. Such a concept of design is denied the classic first-person picaresque narratives of Defoe.

Fielding developed a technique that he had begun to use before, in *Jonathan Wild* and *Joseph Andrews*, of dovetailing motives into an overall plot design. Hence Mrs Miller's cousin Enderson, who turns highwayman (XII. xiv), is made desperate by poverty. His motive, aided by a planned coincidence (meeting Jones on the road and trying to hold him up), prompts Jones' act of charity. When news of Jones' generosity reaches the ears of Mrs Miller – who is impressed, of course – she passes it on together with her other good impressions to Allworthy, who is gradually persuaded to relent in his attitude towards Jones. Enderson's motive is important enough as a social statement. It is less explicit than the concept of 'Give me not poverty lest I steal', as Moll Flanders has it, but no less depressing to contemplate. However, Fielding is not much interested in the social problem, but in creating a catalyst for the plot.

The plot reveals motives that would otherwise be lost or concealed forever. The motives that need no explaining also need no revealing, because they are public in the first place: thus an act of charity is an obvious virtue with a transparent motive, that of wishing to do good. Fielding offers commentary on such occurrences – putting this one down to good nature – but not explanation. Concealed motives are usually, but not always, associated with villainy, malice, sexual favours, and money. Not only do such motives require explanation, they also require signposting. When Tom rescues Molly from the mock-epic battle in the churchyard:

This Accident was luckily owing to Mr. *Square*; for he, Master *Blifil*, and *Jones*, had mounted their Horses, after Church, to take the Air, and had ridden about a Quarter of a Mile, when *Square*, changing his Mind, (not idly, but for a Reason which we shall unfold as soon as we have Leisure) desired the young Gentlemen to ride with him another Way than they had at first purposed. This Motion being complied with, brought them of Necessity back again to the Church-yard. (IV.viii)

Square's motive is revealed eleven chapters later:

Mr. *Square* happened to be at Church, on that *Sunday* when, as the Reader may be pleased to remember, the Appearance of *Molly* in her Sack had caused all that Disturbance. Here he first observed her and was so pleased with her Beauty, that he first prevailed with the young Gentlemen to change their intended ride that Evening, that he might pass by the Habitation of *Molly*, and, by that Means, might obtain a second Chance of seeing her. This Reason, however, as he did not at that time mention to any, so neither did we think proper to communicate it then to the Reader. (V. v)

This passage follows the wonderful tableau in which Square is literally dis-covered when Molly's rug concealing him 'got loose from its Fastning' to reveal, 'among other female Utensils . . . the Philosopher *Square*' in a ridiculous posture (V. v).

This scene reveals two more motives: why Betty Seagrim betrays her sister: jealous hatred of Molly, for stealing the affections of Betty's lover; and why Molly has kept Jones hanging on: like Square, he is a sacrifice 'to her Interest, and to her Pride' (V. vi). Betty's motive enables Jones to get into Molly's bedroom at the opportune moment, and Molly's motive and the discovery of Square let Jones out of the practical dilemma he thought he was in. This sequence of discoveries is integral to the plot, because once Jones knows he is not the father of Molly's child, he is released from the shame heaped upon him by Sophia's discernible (but unspoken) horror. He is also relieved to be released from an obligation to marry Molly.

This pattern of motives – concealed at first, revealed later – serves Fielding's plot well. For instance, no one except Jones goes anywhere without a purpose. Partridge falls in with Jones and agrees to accompany him (VIII. vi). At this stage readers can feel little but sympathy for the unfortunate Partridge, and must be likely to believe him when he tells Jones 'I have loved you ever since I heard of your Behaviour [that is, his honourable generosity] to *Black George*' (VIII. vi). But attentive readers will soon notice the hint that the two men's motives are not in parallel, although until now they have seemed to be. Like all Fielding's heroes, Jones has an inclination to be convivial, so he invites this itinerant barber to share a bottle: for Jones 'was as much pleased with *Partridge*, as *Partridge* could be with him, and had not consulted his own Inclination, but the Good of the other' (VIII. vi). And in the next chapter the author duly reveals 'better Reasons than any which have yet appeared for the Conduct of *Partridge*' (VIII. vi). Harriet Fitzpatrick has a motive for wishing to accompany Sophia that is parallel to Partridge's. Like him, Mrs Fitzpatrick wants to restore child to parent, because she expects a reward for doing so. Both motives are revealed only later, to explain and justify actions that otherwise appear to be founded not on self-interest, but on generosity. This emphasis on motive is important because it focuses attention on human nature rather than incident. Blifil's calculated malice and Tom's impulsive generosity are more important than the actual incidents relating to Sophia's bird (IV. iii). So are the reactions that follow. It is plain that the incident is a vehicle for moral allegory. In addition to such incidents, the whole of the subplot involving Nightingale and Mrs Miller's daughter Nancy is worked seamlessly into the main plot, whilst apparently being there for another purpose. The subplot's function is to highlight Jones' good nature, but it is also an indispensable element of the main plot, because through Nightingale, Allworthy discovers Black George's treachery, and so on.

In these ways, plot can be a vehicle for the revelation of character. Because Fielding warns us that nothing is superfluous to his design, we should expect the interpolated tales, too, to be functional rather than ornamental or digressive. The tales told by the Man of the Hill (VIII. xi–xiv) and by Mrs Fitzpatrick (XI. iv–v) are fictions with an exemplary purpose that may not be immediately self-evident. The stories are of the nature of moral fables. The Man of the Hill recounts his own history, first as a tearaway youth, later as one who learned prudence, only to turn his back on the world. That the youthful Man of the Hill parallels Tom Jones is indisputable, even down to Fielding's phrase describing the two young men: they both have a natural 'Flow of animal Spirits' (VIII. xi, where the Man of the Hill's 'Flow' is 'violent'; IX. v; XIII. v). Similarly, Harriet Fitzpatrick's story is of oppression and elopement, and suggests a parallel with Sophia, except that she has not herself eloped. Since Tom does not (and will not) become a hermit, there is also a contrast between him and his new friend. Since Sophia does not elope, and satisfy her own passions, there is a similar contrast between her and her cousin. (They differ in beauty, too.) The interpolated stories are thematically relevant to the main design, even though the exactness of parallels has sometimes been exaggerated.

Interpolated stories are characteristic of romance, where they are frequently used for little more than ornament. Such stories, in *Joseph Andrews* and *Jonathan Wild*, fit rather uneasily in the whole despite their thematic revelance: they look and sound discursive, even if in fact they are not. In *Tom Jones* the stories are more convincingly and neatly functional. This is true partly because of where they occur in the narrative. The two stories are placed symmetrically on either side of the central episodes at Upton. The Man of the Hill tells a story full of exemplary warnings about moral conduct. No sooner has Tom heard it (with great attentiveness) than he reaches a new moral low, in bed with Jenny Waters/Jones. At Upton, Sophia deserts him. Once on the road, she hears Harriet Fitzpatrick's story. The symmetrical placing of the two stories, with their parallel functions, is a simple and pleasing arrangement that belies the incredible complication of the plot at this point. Fielding organises his characters at Upton in an entanglement which only he can untie. The interpolated tales are also themselves simple, morally and narratively: their simplicity is a foil to the fantastic complications of plot, itself in turn constructed around a basic story that is remarkably simple. After all, the basis of the plot is that Jones the foundling is expelled from home and – unable by his low birth to marry the girl he loves – travels (with adventures) to London, where once the true circumstances of his birth are happily revealed, he can and does marry the girl he loves. Jack has his Jill and they live happily ever after. This is the slight basis, from the stock of romance, on which Fielding builds a plot-structure of astonishing and complex ingenuity.

The ingenuity of the whole, and the happy comedy of the resolution, tend to conceal the profound conservatism of *Tom Jones*. It has been noticed before that no one, not even Jones, ever once questions the social convention which bars him from marriage to Sophia because of his low birth and his presumed bastardy. If there is to be a resolution at all, Jones must be restored to his 'rightful' social status and its accompanying inheritance. By making Jones a gentleman after all, Fielding ultimately protects the rights of that society to treat foundlings as irrelevant to a landed estate and disregard their emotions accordingly. Fielding's – and Tom's – acceptance of the social world he describes with such panache suggests that Tom is no rebel. It is after all hardly rebellious to fall in love with someone you cannot marry. As an eighteenth-century young lady, Sophia has only one rebellious option open to her: to disobey her father. This one parallel between Sophia and Clarissa has often been remarked. Arnold Kettle says that Tom and Sophia do actively rebel, that they fight (unlike Clarissa) with any weapon that comes to hand. He goes on to say that it is not the contrived happy ending, but their cheerful ability to grapple with their situation, that persuades us to 'accept' *Tom Jones*. Sophia has no intention of hanging around at home in order to be forced into marriage with the odious Blifil, so she arranges, quickly and decisively, to leave. But is Tom as active? Were he to pursue Sophia 'by any base or treacherous Method' he would injure Western and worry Allworthy: these 'were Circumstances that tormented him all Day, and haunted him on his Pillow at Night. His Life was a constant Struggle between Honour and Inclination, which alternately triumphed over each other in his Mind' (V. vi). Rather than rebel against the system and indulge his own passion, he decides he must abandon Sophia, not elope with her.

While Fielding does seem at times to be standing up for the rights of young people to marry for love rather than for estates, it is estates he finally gives them. The contrived happy ending is crucial because it affirms the ultimate nature of romantic comedy: it reflects a world that is stable and ordered, unquestioning and unquestioned. If his comedy is therefore optimistic, what can be done about villains? If *Tom Jones* were realistic, that question might be asked with more conviction. But since the thrust of the novel is exemplary rather than realistic, the fate of the villains becomes more a hypothetically moral or philosophical issue than a genuinely practical one. Although this issue is more complex in *Tom Jones*, it is essentially the same as in *Jonathan Wild*: the virtuous cannot expect to survive in the real world unless they learn to recognise their enemies, the villains. In *Jonathan Wild*, the Heartfrees are scarcely serious examples of virtue to be recommended or imitated. At the end of *Tom Jones*, the virtuous characters are equipped with an ability (and enough money) to come to terms with the world. However, they choose actually to have little to do with it, as they are finally distributed in a configuration which keeps them together on their own property in the west country, where they are insulated from the outside world.

The mediator between characters and readers, whose hand arranges that final configuration, is the most celebrated of Fielding's narrators. The chatty narrator of *Joseph Andrews* purports to know the characters and only record their story. The talkative narrator of *Tom Jones* admits once that he has similarly limited power.

To describe every Particular, and to relate the whole Conversation of the ensuing Scene, is not within my Power, unless I had forty Pens, and could, at once, write them all together, as the Company now spoke.   (VII. xii)

This effectively conjures up a charming image of the author himself in the midst of a crowded room, involved in spite of himself. If it does nothing else, his admission creates a dramatic immediacy. However, this is not his usual role. The narrator is no mere observer in a crowd, but one who is privileged to be 'admitted behind the Scenes of this great Theatre of Nature' (VII. i), who has access to 'those secret spontaneous Emotions of the Soul, to which Reason is often a Stranger' (XI. iii). But although he is in a better position than his characters to see into people's minds, yet he occasionally behaves like one of his characters. For instance, he is almost surrealistically in love with Sophia, and has affection for Jones. When Jones lies in prison, the narrator ruefully 'almost despair[s] of bringing him to any good' (XVII. i). We see through such irony, of course, because he has taught us that the design is in his control. There are some moments when this narrator really seems to be Fielding: in one disquisition, authors (he says) feel that their books are their children, and critics who disparage the book disparage the author (XI. i). Contemporary critical practice would identify the narrator with the author. On the whole, however, this narrator is a fictionalised Fielding in much the same way as Sophia is a fictionalised Charlotte Cradock (IV. ii), Fielding's first wife, and Allworthy a fictionalised Allen or Lyttelton. The narrator is, some say, a character in his own novel. He is a guide and companion to the other characters as he is to his readers.

In kind, this narrator is scarcely different from that of *Joseph Andrews*. In degree he is entirely different, for in *Tom Jones* he is ubiquitous. Each one of the eighteen books of *Tom Jones* opens with a chapter addressed by the narrator directly to us, his readers. He explains and qualifies, philosophises or just muses, reflects and cautiously predicts. And the abstractions and generalisations are, of course, his. The style he adopts is certainly familiar. Making the same assumption about his readers' sensitivity as he did in *Jonathan Wild*, he repeats exactly the same expression: as Molly's rug falls from the nail, it reveals '(with Shame I write it, with Sorrow will it be read) – the Philosopher *Square*' (V. v). The same verbal formula occurs when, drunk for joy at Allworthy's recovery from mortal illness (only a chill, actually), Jones is about to take Molly into the bushes. By the third time, when Jones can be found in Mrs Waters' bed, our narrator need no longer tell us that his words will be read with sorrow and he gives us just the first half of the formula. Fielding is entirely in command, so that he knows that his readers will oblige him.

This kind of assuredness, while never extreme enough to be cocky, is relaxed and amusing. On the surface, it contrasts delightfully with another of his characteristic ruses. One of the novel's many 'fierce contentions' begins in the bedroom between Jones and Fitzpatrick: 'And now Mrs. *Waters* (for we must confess she was in the same Bed) being, I suppose, awakened from her Sleep, and seeing two Men fighting in her Bed-chamber, began to scream' (X. ii). The coyly innocent irony of 'I suppose' is also thoroughly assured. It is a hallmark of Fielding's narrative technique in *Tom Jones*. Like the earlier narrators, this one frequently declines to be any firmer: 'I shall not determine' is one of his most overworked expressions. Called upon to account for motives, he is frequently content to offer one concrete suggestion or, evasively, 'some other reason'. He is coy in other ways: some of Squire Western's oaths are 'too shocking to repeat' (for example, VI. vii), and 'Mr. *Jones* being now returned to his own Bed (but from whence he returned we must beg to be excused from relating)' (X. vi). Fondness is 'immoderate' and passions 'violent', but tenderness is inexpressible, so he does not express it. When Sophia learns of Tom's attachment to her through Honour's report of his comments about her muff, we hear: 'Till something of a more beautiful Red than Vermilion be found out, I shall say nothing of *Sophia*'s Colour on this Occasion' (IV. xiv), and at the end of the scene: 'As to the present Situation of her Mind, I shall adhere to a Rule of *Horace*, by not attempting to describe it, from Despair of Success. Most of my Readers will suggest it easily to themselves, and the few who cannot, would not understand the picture, or at least would deny it to be natural, if ever so well drawn' (IV. xiv). Such self-effacement is conventional rhetoric. Usually addressing one reader (male) at a time, he repeats at regular and frequent intervals that his reader is 'sagacious', thus teasing us to be ever more alert to his hints. This is also a form of flattery, or something close to an experience shared between author and reader. Fielding must have felt certain of the kind of audience who would read him: his tentativeness is a pure feint. Only a man who is sure of his readers can tell them how they are bound to respond.

The narrator also lists his own virtues: he has a good heart (IX. i);
he can be trusted because he is truthful (for example, IX. v; IX. vii;
X. ix); these are also customary attributes of the rhetor. But this
narrator is also hospitable: he invites us in at the very beginning of
the novel to partake of a feast, whose menu contains 'a Provision
[of] HUMAN NATURE' (I. i). This feast is likened to that of a 'public
Ordinary' (a cheap restaurant) rather than 'a private or
eleemosynary Treat', which gives the recipient no choice.
'Eleemosynary' is an arresting word, liable to send most readers
(also in 1749) to a dictionary. It means 'charitable'. Its
conspicuousness in the first sentence of the novel is not without a
purpose. The opening shows that, like the best of his characters, the
narrator displays generosity and a special kind of charity, which
takes account of the wishes of the recipient of the charity. The
repeated imagery of eating and refreshment reminds us principally
of his good-natured hospitality towards us, his readers, for whose
welfare, as always, he is solicitous. These qualities help to make him
much more than a conventional rhetorical speaker: the whole
character of the narrator is Fielding's own distinctive creation.

The narrator's voice is so pervasive that his style is largely the
novel's style. Like his predecessors, he cares little for linguistic
misuse. An everyday hyperbole – when a guide tells Jones and
Partridge it is not possible they are lost, although they are – is
likened to the folly of using 'infinite' to mean 'a Distance of half a
Yard' and 'eternal' to mean 'a Duration of five Minutes' (XII. xi).
Although Fielding's objections to linguistic abuse of this sort are less
conspicuous in *Tom Jones* than in his earlier writing, the jargon of
doctors, lawyers, and politicians again receives its share of ridicule,
usually followed by bathetic explanation of the previously
obfuscated obvious. This is one typical element of the narrative
style. For example:

An antient Heathen would perhaps have imputed this Disability to the God
of Drink, no less than to the God of War; for, in Reality, both the
Combatants had sacrificed as well to the former Deity as to the latter. To
speak plainly, they were both dead drunk . . . (IX. vi)

AURORA now first opened her Casement, *anglicè*, the Day began to break,
when *Jones* walked forth . . . (IX. ii)

The kind of bathos quoted here is a stylistic joke at the expense of the
hyperbole of classical similes. 'To speak plainly', 'in plain English',
'in the English phrase', 'in plain Language', 'in simple Phrase':
these and like expressions are typical. They form an ironic reminder

that this is 'a new Province of Writing', since the older, hollow, and alien linguistic conventions are thus ridiculed. Usually Fielding is reducing the language of poetry to prose; the characteristic note of this style is, simply, mockery.

Another significant aspect of narrative style carried over from his earlier fiction is his habit of alluding to paintings or other representational forms of art. Fielding's tributes to his friend William Hogarth are well known. One conspicuous instance is that Bridget Allworthy is said to look like one of Hogarth's comic caricatures, 'in His Print of a Winter's Morning, of which she was no improper Emblem' (I. xi). In such a case, we are not asked to make any effort of imagination to picture her to ourselves. Perhaps more surprisingly, Fielding uses a similar technique to present his heroine Sophia, by having his readers call to mind society portraits, literary descriptions, or any personal image of beauty. Two ludicrous introductory paragraphs simultaneously undercut his own seriousness and mock the 'Elevation of Stile, and all other Circumstances proper to raise the Veneration of our Reader' (IV. ii). Yet he places Sophia in the very convention he mocks, so that any 'Veneration' we may have for her is constantly ironised. We are invited to imagine her:

Reader, perhaps thou hast seen the Statue of the *Venus de Medicis*. Perhaps, too, thou hast seen the Gallery of Beauties at *Hampton-Court*. Thou may'st remember *each bright* Churchill *of the Gallaxy*, and all the Toasts of the *Kit-Cat*. Or if their Reign was before thy Times, at least thou hast seen their Daughters, the no less dazling Beauties of the present Age; whose Names, should we here insert, we apprehend they would fill the whole Volume.

Now if thou hast seen all these, be not afraid of the rude Answer which Lord *Rochester* once gave to a Man, who had seen many Things. No. If thou hast seen all these without knowing what Beauty is, thou hast no Eyes; if without feeling its Power, thou hast no Heart.

Yet is it possible, my Friend, that thou mayest have seen all these without being able to form an exact Idea of *Sophia*: for she did not exactly resemble any of them. She was most like the Picture of Lady *Ranelagh*; and I have heard more still to the famous Dutchess of *Mazarine*; but most of all, she resembled one whose Image can never depart from my Breast, and whom, if thou dost remember, thou hast then, my Friend, an adequate Idea of *Sophia*.

(IV. ii)

All this is by way of introducing the description of Sophia's appearance. It is noticeable that Fielding or his narrator refuses to take this convention seriously. Sophia is beautiful, but the allusion to the Restoration poet Rochester, particularly, introduces a note of scepticism, since the 'rude Answer' was: ' "If you have seen all this, then kiss mine A[rs]e" '. Before we reach the lengthy description of Sophia's 'beautiful Frame' (and her equally beautiful mind), we have in our minds the idioms of literary convention and portrait painting, but predominantly the latter, to imagine her beauty for ourselves. The other allusions in these and subsequent paragraphs include the bride from Suckling's 'Ballad Upon a Wedding', Donne's Elizabeth Drury, from *The Second Anniversarie*, Fielding's own dead wife Charlotte Cradock, and numerous portraits of celebrated society ladies of the early years of the eighteenth century. This is an entirely static set piece.

As with Fanny in *Joseph Andrews*, now with Sophia, Fielding is careful not to make her perfect, even though he calls her 'this Paragon' (IV. ii). If she were entirely perfect, she would be placed beyond the psychological aspiration of any man. She is the more plausible because envy would say that her forehead was too low and her chin 'perhaps' slightly too large: minor they may be, but these are imperfections. She is not an image of perfect beauty, to be sure. Yet Sophia is described for us with a succession of empty or obsolete similes. In her neck 'was Whiteness which no Lillies, Ivory, nor Alabaster could match. The finest Cambric might indeed be supposed from Envy to cover that Bosom, which was much whiter than itself, – It was indeed, *Nitor splendens Pario marmore purius*. "A Gloss shining beyond the purest Brightness of *Parian* Marble" '. With an equally well-tried metaphor, her black eyes shine with 'a Lustre in them, which all her Softness could not extinguish' (IV. ii) and her 'Complexion had rather more of the Lilly than of the Rose' (IV. ii). The total effect of such a description is to suggest that Sophia herself is real. However, her beauty tends to be an abstraction, because it can be expressed only through the hollowest accepted conventions of literary description and of fashionable formal portraiture. Both conventions create an image of the goddess who is almost always a conscious idealisation of a real but slightly imperfect woman.

Fielding creates a parallel effect when he uses theatrical techniques to present particular scenes. These are familiar from his other fiction, too. He makes much of the tableau: probably the best example in *Tom Jones* is Jones' discovery of Square in Molly's bedroom. And some of the poses adopted by his characters are of the kind printed in acting manuals. The statue of surprise, which occurs in *Joseph Andrews* (I. viii), is one example of stylised gesture that is repeated in *Tom Jones*. It occurs in the scene where Tom and Sophia meet at Lady Bellaston's. Here we encounter the attributes of a theatrical scene: it reads rather like a sequence of stage directions:

Sophia expecting to find no one in the Room, came hastily in and went directly to a Glass which almost fronted her, without once looking towards the upper End of the Room, where the Statue of *Jones* now stood motionless. – In this Glass it was after contemplating her own lovely Face, that she first discovered the said Statue; when instantly turning about, she perceived the Reality of the Vision: Upon which she gave a violent Scream, and scarce preserved herself from fainting, till *Jones* was able to move to her, and support her in his Arms. (XIII. xi)

This is followed, characteristically, by an expression of the author's sham inability: 'To paint the Looks or Thoughts of either of these Lovers is beyond my Power' (XIII. xi). The stage-managed type of scene is pervasive. One thinks of Honour not noticing Sophia's blushes because she is too preoccupied with her own image in the mirror (most of Fielding's women find mirrors irresistible); or the confrontation between Mrs Wilkins and Allworthy when the foundling is discovered in the squire's bed; or Sophia's undignified fall from her horse in the yard of 'a very fair promising Inn' (XI. ii; we are rebuked for laughing at this: a pleasing reminder that the novel is *social* discourse). This is a context in which Fielding's experience as a playwright is of obvious relevance.

Just as the characters in his plays speak a 'literary' language rather than a naturalistic one, so the characters in *Tom Jones* are inclined to speak according to the conventions of their literary or theatrical situation. In the scene from which I have quoted where Tom and Sophia meet, the dialogue which eventually gets started, as in most scenes between them, is full of formal professions of ardent admiration, respect, and the like. In the presence of Sophia or Allworthy, Jones spends an inordinate proportion of his time on his knees, begging pardon or professing a desire to serve, and then weeping manly tears at their goodness. Meanwhile Sophia, ever sweet and gracious, expresses nothing more abandoned than the most earnest desires, a natural modesty, and due deference to the male sex. Nothing that Tom and Sophia actually say to each other conveys the idea that they are passionately in love. Tom is more passionate with Sophia's muff than he ever is with Sophia herself, but his rapture speaks eloquently of his devotion to her. Niceties of social convention demand that they keep their passions to themselves when in public: but no one can read this novel without knowing that Tom and Sophia are in love. Their dialogue may be formal, conventional, and hollow, but Fielding lets us know by their sighs, blushes, and glances; by what they are prepared to do for each other; and by what they think: he also simply tells us directly that these two young people are in love.

Theirs is not the only register of language, of course. Thwackum and Square engage for the most part in theological disputes that sound (as indeed they are) bookish. When Jones discovers Square in Molly's closet wearing only a nightcap, Square's 'philosophical' language is entirely in character, but – in the circumstances – entirely ridiculous. Allworthy's colourless prose might represent sweet reason and fair (though more often prejudiced) judgment, but his repeated sermon-lectures are sometimes addressed to closed – or just bored – ears. He seems to speak a written language.

All this suggests that, like character and gesture, dialogue also is stylised in the interests of caricature. But there are exceptions. The astonishingly garrulous Honour speaks with so little regard for rhetorical punctuation that even the gentle Sophia (unable to get a word in edgeways) must resort to a gentle rebuke. Although the talkative maid is no unfamiliar figure in the literature of the period, Honour's speech is authentic in its very garrulity. Also, Squire Western's apparently colloquial west-country idiom is far closer to natural speech, even if his range of similes is severely limited – to comparisons with his hunting dogs. The quasi-phonetic spellings of his words, his colloquial oaths, the violence of his language, match his ebullient temperament perfectly: these make Western the speaker of a raw English that is far too gruff to be conventionalised or 'literary'. Yet Western is still a type, as much as Honour.

The most elusive character in this respect is Blifil. A naturally devious politician, he has no linguistic style of his own, but, like other time-servers he adapts his register to the expectations he thinks his audience will have. Blifil is in fact very careful about his language and, when he gets into a tricky situation, he simply shuts his mouth: he

had Address enough at sixteen to recommend himself at one and the same Time to both these Opposites [that is, Thwackum and Square]. With one he was all Religion, with the other he was all Virtue. And when both were present, he was profoundly silent, which both interpreted in his Favour and in their own. (III. v)

But Blifil is still cleverer than this. Impelled by his 'Zeal . . . inspired with the Love of Justice', that is, his determination to have Black George and the hated Jones removed, Blifil

had forgot the Distance of Time. He varied likewise in the Manner of the Fact; and, by the hasty Addition of the single Letter S, he considerably altered the Story; for he said *George* had wired Hares. These Alterations might probably have been set right, had not Master *Blifil* unluckily insisted on a Promise of Secrecy from Mr. *Allworthy*, before he revealed the Matter to him . . .   (III. x)

This is only one of the many insidious, carefully selected hints that the villain drops in Allworthy's ear. We speak of Blifil's language, although most of his words, as here, are reported, not quoted. This way Fielding reveals Blifil's strategy of hypocrisy more effectively than perhaps he could with direct speech plus authorial commentary. When Allworthy himself eventually calls Blifil a 'wicked Viper' at the end (XVIII. viii), he confirms that this was the serpent in Paradise Hall who brought about the fall of Jones. Allworthy's epithet is his response to another instance of Blifil's lying with the 'Words of Truth' (XVIII. viii; and VII. vi), a form of equivocation that Fielding scornfully proves to be hypocrisy, not the 'Salvo for his Conscience' that Blifil likes to think it is. Blifil's hatred, lust, malice, greed, and treachery make him an archetypal villain; his ability to make his language equivocal equips him the more aptly to become a Methodist and to buy – of all things – a seat in Parliament (XVIII. xiii). Blifil's antithesis is Jones, who is incapable of equivocation: for instance, when spotted in the thicket by Thwackum, Jones defiantly refuses to tell his pompous teacher the name of the 'wicked Slut' he was with. A man of Blifil's linguistic turn would equivocate. The antithesis between Jones and Blifil is a part of a much broader antithetical style: a combination of opposites that shapes the whole novel.

Antithesis is prominent in several ways. We might think of Fielding's satirical exposure of the hypocrites, Thwackum and Square, by whose different opinions of the 'sublime Virtue' of justice, '*Thwackum* would probably have destroyed one half of Mankind, and *Square* the other half' (III. x). More generally, as young Tom rises in one person's affections, he falls in another's; when Allworthy 'plainly saw Master *Blifil* was absolutely detested . . . by his own Mother, he began, on that Account only, to look with an Eye of Compassion upon him' and when he saw Tom rising in Bridget's estimation, so 'that poor Youth, (however innocent) began to sink in his Affections as he rose in hers' (III. vii). This particular example shows that the antithetical style is more than an ornamental and local linguistic device: it serves to embody antithesis between characters and their actions.

Everyone notices how the characters in *Tom Jones* are arranged so often in balancing pairs, such as Tom and Sophia, Thwackum and Square, Partridge and Honour, Allworthy and Western, Lady Bellaston and Lord Fellamar. These pairings shift continually as the characters travel, so that Tom and Partridge are on the road in parallel to Sophia and Honour, and when Tom is with Mrs Waters, Sophia is with Mrs Fitzpatrick. Such symmetrical arrangements make *Tom Jones* in an important sense a schematic novel. There are numerous other, simpler thematic pairings: virtue and vice, for instance, are balanced in Jones himself, and Allworthy is duly pleased with the one and angry with the other (IV. xi). Following the Roman satirist Juvenal, the narrator agrees that virtue and vice co-exist in everyone. This principle is further confirmed in the famous opening to Book XV:

> There are a Set of Religious, or rather Moral Writers, who teach that Virtue is the certain Road to Happiness, and Vice to Misery in this World. A very wholsome and comfortable Doctrine, and to which we have but one Objection, namely, That it is not true. (XV. i)

Other combinations of disparate elements give thematic shape to *Tom Jones*. Benevolence, the natural gift of Allworthy and Jones, runs in constant opposition to the avarice of Blifil, Thwackum, and Square. Jones' love of Sophia is matched by Blifil's hatred of her; Allworthy's hospitality is matched by the ingratitude of his guests. Nature is contrasted with art: in Sophia's appearance, as well as at five country estates, and in Captain Blifil and Square, who are 'artful', while Jones is 'natural'.

The entire narrative strategy of *Tom Jones* is built on the pairing of opposites, a *concordia discors* which explains why the evil are not destroyed, nor even seriously punished. 'For what demonstrates the Beauty and Excellence of any thing, but its Reverse?' (V. i). This is a variation on the traditional argument that we cannot know good without evil: the very definition of one depends on the existence of the other. So in Fielding's outlook, optimism is not an idealism that would (or could) vanquish evil. He pictures a fallen world in which men and women learn practical virtue and learn to protect themselves and their virtue (and their property) against evil.

As long as a Blifil flourishes, Jones – and Allworthy – must learn the same lesson as Adams, Joseph, Fanny, and the Heartfrees: he must learn how to recognise a hypocrite. One of the most powerful single themes of *Tom Jones* is the power of hypocrisy and the difficulty the virtuous and innocent have in overcoming it. The problem is, in Shakespeare's words, that 'There's no art to find the mind's construction in the face'. Appearances deceive. For the innocent abroad, life is a minefield: thus appearances alone convict poor Partridge and cause his early downfall (II. vi). But this is only one aspect of the large theme of appearance and truth. Fielding plays variations on this theme continually.

Time after time, people respond to others on the basis of appearance alone, or appearance accompanied by a smattering of fact, rumour, distorted truth, or downright errors and lies. Hence, with no more than circumstance to go on, the landlord of the Bull's Head at Meriden (if we correctly identify the place so) thinks his beautiful guest is the Pretender's 'mistress', Jenny Cameron, whereas she is the lovely but politically uncommitted Sophia. Fielding's narrator even offers us a little lecture on the justifiable ease with which we fall into suspicion when circumstances encourage us to suspect – even though we do not have all the facts (XI. x). The ultimate proof of error seems to be Jones' behaviour at the masquerade, where he never once knows whose face really is behind the mask. Because he thinks he knows, he mistakes Lady Bellaston for Mrs Fitzpatrick and blunders into an indiscretion. But Jones is too naive even to play the hypocrite, so that he neglects to feign sickness when Lady Bellaston visits him (XV. vii). The truth is, as Partridge observes during Garrick's performance of *Hamlet*: 'How People may be deceived by Faces! *Nulla fides fronti* is, I find, a true Saying' (XVI. v). On the one occasion when Blifil cannot control his face, his blush confirms his guilt – to us, and to Mrs Miller, but not to Allworthy, who is unimpressed by appearances of that sort: responding to a different kind of evidence, he wants to know instead why Blifil 'hesitates' to answer (XVIII. v). Throughout *Tom Jones*, appearances deceive.

Sophia's clumsy attempt to conceal her love of Jones merely confirms her aunt's erroneous suspicions that she loves Blifil (VI. iii). Aunt Western recognises the value of a little 'polite' hypocrisy (VI. v). Wherever she goes, Sophia is, quite correctly, taken for a lady. Similarly, Jones 'was very well dressed, and was naturally genteel, he had a remarkable Air of Dignity in his Look, which is rarely seen among the Vulgar, and is indeed not inseparably annexed to the Features of their Superiors' (VII. xi). Social status does not actually determine his air, which is natural to him, but most people assume he is a gentleman. Jones is treated with the fawning servility typical of Fielding's innkeepers who think of profit, but landladies alter their demeanour when the man they took for 'a Person of Quality' turns out to have very little money (for example, VIII. ii, viii).

One landlady in particular changes her mind from one extreme to another, for having realised Jones has not got much cash on him, she tells the mildly fraudulent doctor that 'every Thing is not what it looks to be. He is an arrant Scrub, I assure you' (VIII. iii). There are dozens of examples of this theme. Jones tells Partridge, 'as you have found me out to be a comical Fellow, so I have no Skill in Physiognomy, if you are not one of the best-natured Gentlemen in the Universe' (VIII. iv). Although Partridge has a certain degree of good nature, Jones has misread that physiognomy and soon afterwards assigns the wrong motive to Partridge's fidelity (and mistakes his Jacobite sentiments for Hanoverian loyalty).

Jones must learn the ability to see through appearances:

To say the Truth, there are but two Ways by which Men become possessed of this excellent Quality. The one is from long Experience, and the other is from Nature; which last, I presume, is often meant by Genius, or great natural Parts; and it is infinitely the better of the two, not only as we are Masters of it much earlier in Life, but as it is much more infallible and conclusive: For a Man who hath been imposed upon by ever so many, may still hope to find others more honest; whereas he who receives certain necessary Admonitions from within, that this is impossible, must have very little Understanding indeed, if he ever renders himself liable to be once deceived. As *Jones* had not this Gift from Nature, he was too young to have gained it by Experience; for at the diffident Wisdom which is to be acquired this Way, we seldom arrive till very late in Life; which is perhaps the Reason why some old Men are apt to despise the Understanding of all who are a little younger than themselves. (VIII. vii)

This is conceptually and verbally very close to Fielding's statement about the character of Heartfree. Although Jones still has very much to learn in this respect, he knows the principle when he tells the Man of the Hill that 'Appearances . . . are often deceitful; Men sometimes look what they are not' (VIII. x). He, at length, replies: 'I have read that a good Countenance is a Letter of Recommendation' (VIII. x).

Only prudence – practical wisdom – enables anyone, good or bad, to recognise the truth behind the appearance of a person's face.

Prudence and Circumspection are necessary even to the best of Men. They are indeed as it were a Guard to Virtue, without which she can never be safe. It is not enough that your Designs, nay that your Actions are intrinsically good, you must take Care they shall appear so. If your Inside be never so beautiful, you must preserve a fair Outside also. This must be constantly looked to, or Malice and Envy will take Care to blacken it so, that the Sagacity and Goodness of an *Allworthy* will not be able to see through it, and to discern the Beauties within. Let this, my young Readers, be your constant Maxim, That no Man can be good enough to enable him to neglect the Rules of Prudence; nor will Virtue herself look beautiful, unless she be bedecked with the outward Ornaments of Decency and Decorum. And this Precept, my worthy Disciples, if you read with due Attention, you will I hope, find sufficiently enforced by Examples in the following Pages.(III. vii)

But Blifil's face can never warn anyone of his 'Inside', not least because he has Wild's expert control over his facial muscles. For so much of the novel, Fielding's emphasis falls on the problem of the outside and the inside character of a human being. Where the outside matches the inside, thus where a handsome face conceals a handsome mind, or a radiant countenance conceals a generous disposition, the result is a perfect harmony and a virtuous character. But vicious characters do not wear vicious faces, of course; they have deceptive appearances of virtue, or good looks, or both. The hypocrite Square, after all, is handsome and sexually attractive. Blifil could not do the damage he does without an outward appearance of virtue (but not handsomeness). Where the outside does not match the inside, the result is usually a vicious or morally unattractive character. Recent research in social psychology has confirmed Fielding's intuition: 'We do judge a book by its cover and a person by his looks. If we don't know very much about someone, our interpretations of his character tend to be consistent with the feelings aroused by his appearance. A beautiful person supposedly has beautiful qualities.'[1]

There is only one prudence, but it is protean. Added to the temperament of Blifil, Thackum, or Square, prudence means self-serving, feathering one's own nest, and destroying the opposition. Therefore prudence is a worldly wisdom, which can serve evil nature. However, added to good nature, prudence protects virtue

---

[1] Leonard Berkowitz, *A Survey of Social Psychology* (Hinsdale, Ill., 1975), p. 180 .

and creates justice tempered with mercy. By contrast, Blifil has little mercy and much justice, and Thwackum and Square (however much they talk) have neither (III. x). It is also pragmatically important that a prudent good-natured person cannot easily be imposed on, and should recognise hypocrisy. Armed with guarded simplicity, Sophia successfully resists Lord Fellamar (XV. v), and long before that she recognises Blifil for the sneaking, base, treacherous rascal he is (IV. v), but no one else does. Prudence therefore intensifies, pragmatically, good or evil nature, and is a practical necessity, not an amiable virtue.

As in his earlier fiction, Fielding's narrator is an agent of Providence who distributes justice to all his characters. When Jones is at his lowest pitch of fortune, in prison, the narrator makes it entirely clear that Jones is responsible for his actions: 'such are the Calamities in which he is at present involved, owing to his Imprudence' (XVII. i). But as for Sophia, 'it is more than probable, that we shall somewhere or other provide a good Husband for her in the End, either *Blifil*, or my Lord, or [with a verbal trick we now recognise] Somebody else' (XVII. i). Then in consecutive sentences, the narrator leaves Jones in prison where his imprudence has got him, yet promises to get him out, saying so with customary irony:

Thus I faithfully promise, that notwithstanding any Affection which we may be supposed to have for this Rogue, whom we have unfortunately made our Heroe, we will lend him none of that supernatural Assistance with which we are entrusted, upon Condition that we use it only on very important Occasions. If he doth not therefore find some natural Means of fairly extricating himself from all his Distresses, we will do no Violence to the Truth and Dignity of History for his Sake; for we had rather relate that he was hanged at *Tyburn* (which may very probably be the Case) than forfeit our Integrity, or shock the Faith of our Reader. (XVII. i)

Although he may say he prefers the probable to the marvellous, his matrix of coincidences and his own vaunted design make 'probability' a very flexible concept indeed. Were he to acquire prudence while in prison, Jones would just take his prudence with him to the gallows, where it would be unlikely to do him much good. There is therefore nothing that Jones can do to change his own fate: that is in the hands of the agent of Providence. The moral and didactic nature of the narrator's comments forces us to realise that Jones learns from his experience. However, he can escape, because this is fiction. The rest of us take note: our imprudence would not be so readily forgiven. If Jones learns prudence, Providence will save him, then, for two reasons: he will have learned to be morally responsible for his own actions, and he is good-natured enough to deserve saving.

The key virtues of *Joseph Andrews*, chastity and charity, have their parts to play in this novel, too, but charitable Tom Jones is self-evidently not chaste. Equally obviously, unchastity is a venial sin: although Allworthy refuses to take it lightly, Western thinks nothing of it, and Sophia is finally content to dismiss it. Only the rank hypocrites condemn Tom's affair with Molly and then on the specious grounds that he is corrupting her: their real motive is to blacken his moral reputation. Anyway, Square is as unchaste as Jones, and Blifil's sexual appetite considerably unhealthier than either of theirs. Obviously at odds with self-interest, charity is a stronger virtue. In *A Journey from this World to the Next* the gates of Elysium fly open instantly to admit the charitable. Fielding obviously considered charity a most important virtue; it is the pragmatic product, perhaps the proof, of good nature. Good nature is the key to *Tom Jones*.

The happy ending of *Tom Jones* is the contrived and conventional ending of romance, But there is not an exact antithesis of reward and punishment. The good-natured are certainly attractive examples of virtue, whose happiness is itself a reward. But the ill-natured, as examples of vice, are to be avoided on the evidence of their unpleasantness, not because Providence punishes them. By deploying this arrangement, Fielding hints that Providence is a benign deity. He also puts his subject in a perspective that just takes the edge off a glib distribution of reward and punishment. For although the good-natured are brought together and rewarded, the evil-natured are not exactly punished. Blifil does not get what he wants, but neither is he consigned to any dire future. None of the ill-natured is executed or imprisoned, nor is any condemned to abject poverty: these might have been forms of fictional punishment. Instead (with the exception of Square, who dies soon after repenting) they live on in character. Thwackum continues to make 'many fruitless Attempts to regain the Confidence of *Allworthy*, or to ingratiate himself with *Jones*, both of whom he flatters to their Faces, and abuses behind their Backs' (XVIII. xiii). Blifil receives £300 a year, more than enough to live comfortably. Nowhere is there any sign that the evil-natured express remorse for their malice: Blifil's tears, for instance, are not tears of contrition, but of anger that his scheming has been discovered and himself defeated (XVIII. xi).

Ultimately only actions can denote the mind; yet even actions are misinterpreted, usually by observers who know only one motive (that is, what their own would be) and cannot imagine any other. It is still necessary for someone to clear away those misinterpretations, to provide an absolute truth which makes actions unambiguous. That someone is the author. He organises the plot. Under his control, the plot reveals the actions and thus the minds of the characters. The plot is the expertly constructed design of Providence in the world.

5

Amelia

In October 1748, four months before the publication of *Tom Jones*, Fielding had been commissioned Justice of the Peace for the city of Westminster. By January 1749 one of his influential patrons, the Duke of Bedford, had helped him to qualify for the magistracy of the county of Middlesex. The story of Fielding's remarkably effective legal career is outside the scope of this book, except in so far as it affected his writing. Between February 1749, when *Tom Jones* appeared, and December 1751, when *Amelia*, his last novel, was published, Fielding's only other writings were three short pamphlets – all concerned one way or another with legal subjects. Two of them, *A Charge Delivered to the Grand Jury* (1749) and *An Enquiry into the Causes of the Late Increase of Robbers* (1751), focus on social evils – not so much crimes as the causes of criminality – which bring about a state of moral decline in Britain. These pamphlets, as Martin C. Battestin points out in his illuminating introduction to *Amelia*, are indicative of Fielding's changed mood. The realities of his work on the bench were depressing indeed.

In January 1752, immediately after *Amelia*, Fielding began the last of his four periodicals, *The Covent-Garden Journal*, which was issued twice a week until the end of November and contained some of his most interesting essays. How he managed to take time from his daunting schedule as a magistrate to write a lengthy novel, and then run a journal, remains a mystery. Despite his legal duties, he had been writing *Amelia* since about the middle of 1749: towards the end of that year Richardson had heard that 'this fashionable author' was to include scenes set in Newgate in his novel (*Correspondence*, IV, 286). But until the weeks before publication, when advertisements started to appear, almost no one else seems to have known that Fielding was at work on *Amelia*.

By printing 5,000 copies of the first edition, Andrew Millar, Fielding's publisher, expected *Amelia* to sell well, but it proved less successful than he had hoped. Although Millar's inspired advertising and promotion helped the sales to reach a respectable level, there was insufficient demand for a second edition. In fact, the novel was condemned and ridiculed almost from the start. As early as 21 February 1752 Richardson was gloating to his crony Thomas Edwards over the 'disapprobation' that *Amelia* had provoked, and he was not alone in being glad to see Fielding brought down a peg or two after 'the success his spurious brat Tom Jones so unaccountably met with' (*Correspondence*, III, 33–4). By populating his novel with criminals, whores, bailiffs, and pimps, Fielding drew upon himself the charge that *Amelia* was 'low', or not genteel enough. Such criticism – irrelevant now, of course – largely missed the point. But it is significant that *Amelia* posits no moral differences corresponding to differences of social rank: *Joseph Andrews* or *The Beggar's Opera* for that matter had made a similar point. The generous are those who can least afford to be, while the advantages of social eminence seem to encourage vice. The nameless lord, for instance, even indulges in a form of blackmail to satisfy his carnal appetite. But Fielding knew how his readers would respond. He refers to his principal characters, Booth and Amelia, as 'this happy Couple, if the Reader will allow me to call poor People happy' (V, 2), which is less a defiant insult to snobbish readers than an apologetic sign of accepted taste, of what a novel was expected to contain. To this day *Amelia* remains the least popular and least read of Fielding's novels.

Fielding's concern with legal matters, derived inevitably from his experience on the bench, influenced *Amelia* very obviously, since the novel contains so much satire directed against inhumane inequities in the law. Billy Booth, an army officer on half-pay, is always getting into debt and consequently always being confronted by the cruelties of the law. But Fielding's perspective is wide enough to include also the social and, by implication, the political constitution of Britain, so that the corruptions and harsh injustices allowed by the law are seen to be the responsibility of society as a whole. Injustice is thus a moral and social issue, not just a narrowly legal one.

This concern with law makes *Amelia* sound like a new departure for Fielding, though in fact one might argue that the legal system he satirises is another paradigm for the kind of socio-political theme that characterises *Jonathan Wild*. *Amelia* actually resembles *Jonathan Wild* in several respects, particularly where Fielding explores the problems encountered by virtuous people in a hostile world. *Amelia* also resembles other earlier works, notably where Fielding adapted material from four plays: *The Temple Beau*, *The Modern Husband*, *Rape upon Rape: or, the Coffee-House Politician*, and *Don Quixote in England*. Those provide the origins of individual scenes and characters in *Amelia*, the most obvious similarities being between

Squeezum (in *The Coffee-House Politician*) and the trading justice Thrasher, and Lord Richly (in *The Modern Husband*) and the noble lord in *Amelia*. In addition, almost all of Fielding's characters in *Amelia* have counterparts, from which they differ more in degree than in kind, in his earlier fiction: thus Amelia herself resembles Sophia but with much less energy; Booth is Tom Jones without the youthful or romantic appeal; honest Serjeant Atkinson is a stiffer version of Joseph Andrews; pious Dr Harrison a kind of Abraham Adams without the comic verve; and so on. All these pairings suggest that *Amelia*'s characters are created either with staginess or with less vitality than before. The relative dullness of the characters is one reason why *Amelia* has few ardent admirers.

There are other reasons for *Amelia*'s failure to please. One theory, that Fielding's imaginative gifts had deserted him, takes too little account of the creative energy of his other late writings. Another rather more plausible view is that his new preoccupation with social and judicial matters became such an obsession that he was distracted from the need to entertain his readers, in particular to make them laugh. This view suggests that some readers find *Amelia* boring or dry, as indeed some do. A related critical judgment holds that the magistrate allowed his experience to make his novel gloomy and brooding, yet this too overlooks the moments of fun (often forgotten in accounts of *Amelia*) and some comic characterisation as convincing as anything Fielding had written before. Finally, if fainting, swooning, and weeping indicate sentimentality – in a sense that I will qualify later – *Amelia* is one of the most sentimental novels in English. *Amelia* is over-explicit about the emotions involved in pathetic or tragic scenes, emotions with which Fielding hopes some of his readers will sympathise. Novels of sensibility – fashionable enough in the 1750s – win few admirers now.

Critical dismissal of *Amelia* often seems to imply disappointment that it is not like *Tom Jones*. That novel certainly was a hard act to follow, but instead of attempting anything we might call a sequel to his masterpiece, Fielding adopted a new form of realism and changed his narrative technique, setting, and overall tone. *Tom Jones* is loosely an epic, with a plot drawn from romance, while *Amelia* is consciously modelled (at least in part) on a classical epic – Virgil's *Aeneid* – and affects to eschew romance altogether (VIII, 5). In fact, Fielding did exploit romance in *Amelia*, but in so restrained a fashion that he created a domestic epic. Significantly, in contrast to the transparent contrivances of *Tom*

Jones, which ultimately oblige Fielding to resign any serious claim to realism, the majority of *Amelia* is uncompromisingly realistic.

Fielding's realism is nicely underscored by his new attention to detail. He stressed in *Tom Jones* that the great events of history originate in small incidents that are insignificant in themselves. His conception of realism shapes the narrative of *Amelia* through ordinary, minute details with an almost Richardsonian obsessiveness, close to the kind he had preferred to parody twelve years earlier in *Shamela*. At the same time many other details are swept aside as unimportant, uninteresting, or irrelevant. Thus, as in Richardson's fiction, the details are actually seldom gratuitous. For instance, the information that it is 'hashed Mutton' that Amelia lovingly prepares for Booth's dinner turns out to be not at all inconsequential, but emotively charged because it is his favourite dish, which he does not come home to eat because he is out losing money at cards, while she is scrimping (X, 5; and see Rawson,[1] *Henry Fielding and the Augustan Ideal Under Stress*, pp. 90–1). Such minutiae show 'how capable the most insignificant Accident is of disturbing human Happiness, and of producing the most unexpected and dreadful Events. A Reflection which may serve to many moral and religious Uses', not to say fictional ones (IV, 7).

The plot of *Tom Jones* ends with the marriage of the hero and heroine; *Amelia*'s first sentence announces the subject as 'The various Accidents which befel a very worthy Couple, after their uniting in the State of Matrimony.' As John Cleland realised in 1751, Fielding's decision to begin, not end, with a married couple, was 'the boldest stroke that has yet been attempted in this species of writing' (*Critical Heritage*, item 109). Essentially, Fielding deprived himself of the most obvious ready-made plot of romance, because he could not then bring his hero and heroine together at the end in a conventional marriage. What he used instead was a plot that often looks inconsequential and shapeless, whose ending is, however, actually another conventional one from romance: a restored inheritance leading to blissful retreat. Still, on the whole Fielding's self-conscious artifice in *Tom Jones* makes way in *Amelia* for a plot that is neither especially improbable nor minutely contrived.

Just as the narrator of *Tom Jones* speaks of Blifil's omission of only one little material circumstance (III. iv), so the narrator of *Amelia* tells us that a pawnbroker only 'made a small Deviation from the Truth' (XII, 3) – in each case a euphemism for a deliberate lie. *Amelia*'s narrator still gives 'material Hints' to his readers (for example, XII, 3), because they may 'chance' to be relevant later, and he even draws attention to an aside 'after our usual Manner' (I, 2), which suggests continuity with Fielding's previous practice. However, two things have virtually disappeared. One is the celebration of the structure that is contrived and advertised by the narrator. The other is that narrator's jauntiness. The cheerful, chatty narrator is replaced in *Amelia* by a more sombre, enigmatic, and less conspicuous figure, who rarely indulges in witty disquisitions, and whose efforts to excite laughter are fewer and more ponderous than those of his predecessor. In fact, the self-assurance is so muted that it has all but vanished. This, as I shall argue, is a crucial element of the world Fielding is trying to portray and – if he can – come to terms with.

That world is also more restricted, even though we are sometimes taken as far afield as Gibraltar. Most of the narrative is set in a small and mostly seedy area of inner London, and there it remains, without the broad sweep, the panoramic effect of *Tom Jones*. And the irony of *Tom Jones*, which had been a necessary vehicle of that novel's good humour, has been changed, apparently in accordance with Fielding's new, gloomier mood rather than with some decision to avoid mere repetition of a formula for literary success. *Amelia* is frequently ironic, but Fielding's purpose seems far more serious now, as the first words of the dedication – to Ralph Allen – indicate:

> The following Book is sincerely designed to promote the Cause of Virtue, and to expose some of the most glaring Evils, as well public as private, which at present infest the Country; tho' there is scarce, as I remember, a single Stroke of Satire aimed at any one Person throughout the whole. (p. 3)

The main purpose of satire is not usually to amuse, anyway, but the satire of *Amelia* is so serious that it tends to make readers uncomfortable without the safety valve of laughter. The disclaimer in the dedication is a restatement of the contemporary satirist's self-defence: he attacks not the individual but the species. Given the surprising number of rather anonymous characters who people the novel, Fielding's opening paragraph can be taken at face value. The complementary purpose of promoting virtue was only too likely to provoke the contempt of Fielding's readers, as he himself admits twice (IV, 3; XI, 4), and as in fact it did in some quarters.

My purpose in this chapter is not exactly to rehabilitate *Amelia* in view of its generally hostile reception, nor to offer another sustained comparison with *Tom Jones*, but to take the novel on its own terms, in the light of Fielding's stated purpose. *Amelia* is an original novel of satirical protest: indeed, as Martin Battestin rightly says, it 'may be fairly called the first novel of social protest and reform in English' (Introduction to *Amelia*, p. xv), and *Amelia*, not *Tom Jones*, is therefore Fielding's 'new species of writing'. *Amelia* also combines satire and sentiment. Perhaps because it differs from Fielding's other fiction (though much less radically than is sometimes believed), it has been largely misunderstood. *Amelia* is a richer and more rewarding novel than its reputation implies.

II

The opening chapters of *Amelia* are unusually important, because they quickly establish Fielding's main themes and the nature of his narrative, and help determine how his readers will respond. When readers come to Book I, chapter 1, they already know Fielding's purpose, from the dedication. In the first chapter, the narrator introduces himself and his subject. Fielding's earlier narrators were adept at not presuming to determine the truth of this or that point, as this one often is, but here at the beginning there is a subtle difference: the 'Distresses' endured by his 'very worthy Couple'

were some of them so exquisite, and the Incidents which produced these so extraordinary, that they seemed to require not only the utmost Malice, but the utmost Invention which Superstition hath ever attributed to Fortune: Tho' whether there be any such Being in the Universe, is a Matter which I by no Means presume to determine in the Affirmative. (I, 1)

Without the usual tentativeness (transparent as that is) this narrator's position is explicit as he sets out on familiar territory, using Fortune to introduce the theme of Providence. Attentive readers know half-way through this first paragraph that 'Malice' and 'Invention' are human contrivances, and that 'Fortune' is only a convenient word to cover them, like an excuse, as in fact the rest of the paragraph explains. Booth, the 'hero' of the fiction, blames Fortune because he 'imagined, that a larger Share of Misfortunes had fallen to his Lot than he had merited; and this led him, who (tho' a good classical Scholar) was not deeply learned in religious Matters, into a disadvantageous Opinion of Providence' (I, 3). As in *Joseph Andrews* and *Tom Jones*, Providence eventually does rescue Amelia and Booth from distress, through the device of a previously forged will, but this time Fielding draws little attention to his own artifice, allowing his narrator to be more a commentator than a designer. Bursting in with news of the forgery, Dr Harrison exclaims to Booth: 'Your Sufferings are all at an End; and Providence hath done you the Justice at last, which it will one Day or other render to all Men' (XII, 7).

Although less conspicuous than in the previous novels, Providence is still powerful, but Fielding has shifted his emphasis, away from the providential intervention of the author and towards human motivation and responsibility. Early in the novel, Booth's unwillingness to believe in a providential order is: 'A dangerous Way of Reasoning, in which our Conclusions are not only too hasty, from an imperfect View of Things; but we are likewise liable to too much Error from Partiality to ourselves; viewing our Virtues and Vices as through a Perspective, in which we turn the Glass always to our own Advantage, so as to diminish the one, and as greatly to magnify the other' (I, 3). Such a belief encourages vanity, and therefore error. Echoing the philosophical injunction from Pope's *Essay on Man* not to presume to know the whole when we can see only parts, this passage has the structural function of preparing for Booth's continual habit of forming conclusions and judgments based on incomplete evidence, on parts rather than wholes. This is one of the reasons why Booth constantly makes foolish mistakes.

In *Amelia* Fielding therefore approaches one of his favourite themes, but from a different angle: 'To retrieve the ill Consequences of a foolish Conduct, and by struggling manfully with Distress to subdue it, is one of the noblest Efforts of Wisdom and Virtue'. This, he points out, has nothing to do with fortune. It is what he calls the 'ART of LIFE'. His previous virtuous characters, the Heartfrees, Joseph Andrews, Parson Adams, Tom Jones, and others, have to overcome various difficulties – often of their own making – and learn how to live in a hostile world before receiving the rewards of Providence. But this declaration suggests that *Amelia* will not explore the ways in which people can benefit from this experience, but how they prove their virtue.

With these signposts clearly marked, '*The History sets out*' with a curious indifference to details or facts: 'On the first of *April*, in the Year ——, the Watchmen of a certain Parish (I know not particularly which) within the Liberty of *Westminster*, brought several Persons whom they had apprehended the preceding Night, before *Jonathan Thrasher*, Esq; one of the Justices of the Peace for that Liberty' (I, 2). Either the year and the parish are unknown, or the narrator knows them but is not telling: either way, attention must be focused instead on Thrasher, whose name alone suggests the kind of J.P. he is. Like his predecessors, especially in Fielding's drama, Thrasher is demonstrably corrupt and ignorant. And in accordance with Fielding's previous practice, this narrator suspends the narrative almost as soon as it has begun, 'after our usual Manner, [to] premise some Things which it may be necessary for thee to know' (I, 2). These 'Things' are the defects of the law: it is bad enough that trading justices exist, and flourish, but the reason why is that the system lets them.

Here is a good example of Fielding's satiric method. There is no need to appeal to Fielding's experience as a magistrate to explain or justify the appearance of a trading justice. Although Thrasher is based probably on a real, corrupt magistrate, Henry Broadhead, he could be based on any number of examples. But to recognise Thrasher, readers need to know nothing about Broadhead, nor do they even need to have stepped inside a court, because Thrasher is also a caricature who is so familiar from writing of the period (not only Fielding's) that he is representative of a literary species. He is thus a vehicle for satire directed against a legal system so full of loopholes that it entitles a man to dispense law who has 'never read one Syllable of the Matter'. The heavy-handed irony of understatement is there: this corruption of the law is represented by a man who 'had some few Imperfections in his magistratical Capacity', and his monstrous ignorance 'perhaps was a Defect'. His corruptibility, however, is graver. Without a thought for justice, Thrasher indiscriminately condemns people, releases them, or commits them to prison, according to their appearance or how much they can pay him. One of those he commits is Booth, who has tried to prevent a crime, but whose innocence and shabby appearance are enough, in Thrasher's perverted justice, to condemn him. This is the note on which *Amelia* gets started.

Later, when not actually in prison or the sponging house, Booth lives in almost constant fear of arrest for debt: he dares not walk far from his lodgings, since he must not step outside the Verge of the Court, an area in which debtors were safe from arrest. Such safety implies not liberty but a restriction, so that London itself becomes a prison to him. His enemies continually lure him into debts to get him securely out of the way, so that they may pursue their schemes of seducing his beautiful wife, Amelia. This is the real horror. The threat of losing his liberty haunts him: imprisonment is bad enough in itself, but any confinement is terrible for Booth because it parts

him from Amelia. This thought passes through his unhappy mind
when he is carried off to be fleeced at the sponging house:

> The Charms of Liberty against his Will rushed on his Mind; and he could
> not avoid suggesting to himself, how much more happy was the poorest
> Wretch who without Controul could repair to his homely Habitation, and
> to his Family; compared to him, who was thus violently and yet lawfully
> torn away from the Company of his Wife and Children. And their
> Condition, especially that of his *Amelia*, gave his Heart many a severe and
> bitter Pang. (VIII, 1)

The repeated sequence of debt, arrest, and imprisonment always
carries the threat of a journey to Newgate, as the bailiff at this
sponging house chillingly reminds Booth (VIII, 10). Fielding could
have chosen to describe and protest against the notoriously
appalling and inhuman conditions in which prisoners were kept,
but instead he uses Newgate as a microcosm of judgment by
appearance, crime itself, and moral corruption. The Keeper of
Newgate, like Thrasher and Bondum the bailiff, is blithely unaware
of the moral implications of the law and callously indifferent to the
situation of the unfortunate (I, 3). The prisoners are scarcely any
different. Inside Newgate, 'the Dispositions of the other Prisoners
might have induced [Booth] to believe that he had been in a
happier Place: For much the greater part of his Fellow-Sufferers,
instead of wailing and repining at their Condition, were laughing,
singing and diverting themselves with various kinds of Sports and
Gambols' (I, 3). It is hard to know if Fielding expected (or hoped)
that legal punishment should encourage some kind of moral
improvement, but he knew imprisonment in Newgate did nothing
of the sort. Without describing the physical place, he projects the
attitudes it represents: 'the brutalizing *moral* climate of the prison'
and 'the inequities and imperfections of the legal system that
supports it', as Battestin puts it (note to I, 3).

The first thing that happens to Booth inside Newgate is that,
having no money, he is abandoned by the Keeper and stripped of his
coat by way of payment, as if the prison were a hideous parody of an
hotel (and with a humourless euphemistic irony, the Keeper calls
the prisoners his 'Guests' (IV, 2)). Money was customarily extorted
from new prisoners, as an alternative to their being fettered, and to
buy them allegedly comfortable lodging, food, drinks, and other
prisoners' drinks.

Until John Howard's reforms in the 1770s, extortion and
harassment in prisons remained a cause of public outrage (as they

had since at least the later 1720s), but not of effective legislation. They are constant features of *Amelia*, both as subjects on their own for isolated, strident, authorial diatribes (for example, XI, 5, on 'this abominable Practice of touching') and as elements of a debtor's experience of Newgate morality. Like a surgeon or an innkeeper in one of Fielding's earlier novels, the governor of the prison 'with great Dexterity proportioned his Bills to the Abilities of his Guests to pay' (IV, 2). Booth is expected to pay, even for his own arrest and for coach-hire at only 'just double the legal Fare', when he is taken to a sponging house. He is also expected to pay people such as the bailiff's 'Followers', who treat him with 'what they call Civility, that is, they neither struck him nor spit in his Face' (VIII, 1), but who are later ordered by the bailiff to lay 'violent Hands on *Booth*' and take him to Newgate (VIII, 10). Moments later, his bail suddenly assured, Booth prepares to leave the sponging house, when the bailiff and his ruffians have the effrontery to demand 'Civility Money'. Booth refuses to pay them a farthing, and Dr Harrison stoutly declares he would rather see the bailiff punished than rewarded. The bailiff and his men plainly see no moral paradox in what they do, because in their world there is no distinction between treatment and mistreatment: they recognise no moral issue to be discussed. The simple irony points to something peculiarly absurd and cruelly unjust about a system whose custodians are allowed to plunder insolvent debtors and thus force them into even deeper debt. Fielding registers his protest about it.

After his rapid initiation in the customs of the prison, Booth meets prisoners, who come upon him in a quick, bewildering succession, beginning with '*Blear-Eyed Moll;* a Woman of no very comely Appearance'. This character, who vanishes from the novel almost immediately afterwards, is the subject of a caricature that is 'productive of moral Lesson'. She looks totally repellent, degenerate, and diseased:

Her Eye (for she had but one) whence she derived her Nick-name was such, as that Nick-name bespoke; besides which it had two remarkable Qualities; for first, as if Nature had been careful to provide for her own Defect, it constantly looked towards her blind Side; and secondly, the Ball consisted almost entirely of white, or rather yellow, with a little grey Spot in the Corner, so small that it was scarce discernible. Nose she had none; for *Venus*, envious perhaps at her former Charms, had carried off the gristly Part; and some earthly Damsel, perhaps from the same Envy, had levelled the Bone with the rest of her Face: Indeed it was far beneath the Bones of her Cheeks, which rose proportionally higher than is usual. About half a dozen ebeny [*sic*] Teeth fortified that large and long Canal, which Nature had cut from Ear to Ear, at the Bottom of which was a Chin, preposterously short, Nature having turned up the Bottom, instead of suffering it to grow to its due Length.

Her Body was well adapted to her Face; she measured full as much round the middle as from Head to Foot; for besides the extreme Breadth of her Back, her vast Breasts had long since forsaken their native Home, and had settled themselves a little below her Girdle. (I, 3)

The long, leisurely description of a minor character is included because this 'unlovely Creature' had been 'taken in the Fact with a very pretty young Fellow' and 'however wretched her Fortune may appear to the Reader, she was one of the merriest Persons in the whole Prison' (I, 3). Her allegedly merry disposition (for what it is worth) confirms Booth's perception that Newgate is not what it appears. She demands a dram of gin from him, curses him dreadfully when he replies that he has no money, threatens to assault him, and walks off. A few moments later she is seen taking part in a merciless attack on a homosexual inmate, and that is the last we see of her. We learn nothing whatever about Booth's reaction to his brief encounter with Blear-Eyed Moll, so that surprise and shock are not filtered through his consciousness but addressed directly to readers. Grimly funny perhaps, Fielding's vivid comic caricature is not gratuitous. As C. J. Rawson has perceptively commented, the portrait of Blear-Eyed Moll is unique in its 'combination of *extreme* grotesquerie with *so many* reminders of order' (*Henry Fielding and the Augustan Ideal Under Stress*, p. 81). Moll is also mildly shocking, because the description stresses familiar natural proportions and proprieties together with a gross disjunction between her uncommonly hideous appearance and her apparent sexual success with a 'very pretty young Fellow'. Such descriptions, rare in *Amelia*, evince the reduced gaiety of Fielding's style, but Moll's function is still exemplary in much the same way as his earlier conception of character had demanded, particularly when she is seen as a part of the series of prisoners with whom Booth has fleeting contact.

Booth is actually rescued from Moll's imminent physical assault by 'a tall Prisoner', who 'was not himself of the most inviting Aspect', but whose deistic sentiments appeal to Booth. Further, 'something' in his manner 'seemed to distinguish him from the Crowd of Wretches who swarmed in those Regions'. This man – whose name, we learn only when it is casually dropped, is Robinson – takes Booth on a rapid tour of the prison, which awakens his

117

horror, sympathy, and indignation. These scenes have two functions: one satirical, the other a part of Fielding's narrative strategy.

Booth is told that two pitiable wretches are father and daughter, both committed because she stole a loaf of bread to keep him from starving and he accepted it 'knowing it to be stolen'. Her offence is a felony, Robinson explains, and so is not bailable, yet a perjurer is expecting to be released on bail next day. Booth's astonishment that this sort of inequity can occur embodies Fielding's satirical protest against the legal system. The law as applied is unjust and inhumane because it takes no account of mitigating circumstances, and the various executors of the law show what happens when the system is accepted without question. The second function of these scenes has more to do with the relationship between speaker and listener. No sooner has Robinson suggested a game of cards than an anonymous female prisoner denounces him as a cheat and 'a grave looking Man, rather better drest than the Majority of the Company, came up to Mr. *Booth*' to denounce the man's irreligiousness. Although Fielding gives us Booth's warmly indignant responses to the plight of the unfortunate, he does not indicate anything of Booth's reactions to Moll, the deist, or the grave man (who turns out to be a Methodist), so that we have very little sense of Booth's interaction with the people who accost him. His judgment of them – that is, of their appearance – is evidently not very important: ours, as readers, is. The conduct of most prisoners is the opposite of what one might expect; Blear-Eyed Moll has already shown (however absurdly) that appearances can be deceptive; the deist Robinson does indeed turn out (much later) to be a cheat and a crook; and only at the end of the chapter do we discover, when the narrator tells us so, again casually, that the grave Methodist, for all his pious talk, is a pickpocket (I, 4). We cannot know who is telling the truth.

Fielding crammed a lot into his first three chapters. The main business of the novel really starts only when Booth meets his old flame Miss Mathews, who makes a brief appearance at the end of chapter 4. To his surprise, he receives a guinea from an anonymous donor (Miss Mathews, in fact) in chapter 5, and at once loses it at cards to Robinson, who defends his reputation convincingly enough to make Booth begin 'to waver in his Opinion, whether the Character given by Mr. *Robinson* of himself, or that which the others gave of him, was the truer' (I, 5). Booth, then, like Fielding's readers, cannot decide what to believe. The pattern established early in the novel creates doubt about how anyone can trust anyone else: appearance alone is plainly inadequate, but there never seems to be enough other evidence for an accurate assessment. However, this stops no one from making their assessments and drawing their own conclusions, as Thrasher's unjust judgments have already amply proved.

By the time Miss Mathews begins the story of how she came to be committed to Newgate on a charge of murder, which astonishes and horrifies Booth, he ought to be on his guard, but he is too gullible and too easily the victim of his own passion.She is seducing him, as readers realise long before Booth does. That Miss Mathews should not be trusted in any way will emerge as the novel unfolds. In the early chapters Fielding drops enough hints to let us know that Booth is incapable of judging anyone accurately (and he will not be alone in this). Miss Mathews is just another disreputable character who imposes on the innocent and naive.

III

As in his previous fiction, Fielding schematically divides his characters into two distinct categories: the good-natured and ill-natured. The paragon is the heroine, Amelia, whose only imperfection is her injured nose (a source of endless amusement to Fielding's earliest readers). We have heard of her perfections long before she actually appears, because Booth lards his recent life history – reciprocally told to Miss Mathews – with praise of his wife. When she makes her entrance, Amelia comes to take Booth away from prison, thus infuriating Miss Mathews, who has just paid for his release, as well as her own, and who was looking forward to enjoying more 'criminal Conversation' (that is, sex) with him (IV, 2). Amelia rushes in 'all pale and breathless', and promptly faints. Once recovered, she recognises Miss Mathews and commiserates with her on her imprisonment. The contrast between these two could not be more marked. Miss Mathews expects to be roundly insulted by a jealous wife, but Amelia's 'Virtue could support itself with its own intrinsic Worth, without borrowing any Assistance from the Vices of other Women; and she considered their natural Infirmities as the Objects of Pity, not of Contempt or Abhorrence' (IV, 2). Amelia is sweetness and light. Miss Mathews, however, is cold and reserved, because

besides that her Spirits were entirely disconcerted by so sudden and unexpected a Disappointment; and besides the extreme Horrors which she conceived at the Presence of her Rival, there is, I believe, something so

119

outrageously suspicious in the Nature of all Vice, especially when joined with any great Degree of Pride, that the Eyes of those whom we imagine privy to our Failings, are intolerable to us, and we are apt to aggravate their Opinions to our Disadvantage far beyond Reality. (IV, 2)

In this baldest of comparisons, Amelia is virtuous and innocent, Miss Mathews vicious and guilty. The novel will later introduce more characters parallel to Miss Mathews, whose guilt only intensifies their vice, 'so much more quick-sighted . . . is Guilt than Innocence' (VI, 2): at least they have consciences. The contrast is complete at the very end, when, unlike Amelia, who remains slim and attractive, Miss Mathews has become 'very disagreeable in her Person, and immensely fat' (XII, 9).

Plainly, Miss Mathews holds Amelia in contempt, thinking her credulous rather than honest (II, 2): it is typical of Fielding's unpleasant characters that they never believe anyone else can be honest, because they themselves are not. Yet Amelia's potential seducers all recognise her virtue as a source of sexual attraction, as if it exists only to be destroyed. According to Mrs Atkinson, men prefer a challenge to an easy conquest: ' "Good Heavens! what are these Men! What is this Appetite, which must have Novelty and Resistance for its Provocatives; and which is delighted with us no longer than while we may be considered in the Light of Enemies" ' (VII, 9).

Amelia's virtue also maddens her female rivals. There is a very thin line between her virtue and prudishness, and it is jealousy, disappointment, or a combination of those with alcohol that makes others insult her as a prude (III, 9; X, 8). Before she makes her first appearance in the narrative Amelia's virtues have been lauded so much – by Booth, Dr Harrison, and just general report, that like the heroines of sentimental drama, her perfections are established without her having to prove them. But then she does go on to prove them, repeatedly, for the remaining two-thirds of the novel.

In the exercise of her virtue, Amelia is certainly different from Fanny or Sophia, neither of whom consistently *displays* virtue as Amelia does. Fielding uses her explicitly to defend such unfashionable things as motherhood, love, marriage, goodness, and generosity against the expected contempt of the scoffers among his readers. He includes Amelia's sentimental homily – to her six-year-old son – on love, goodness, and the bad people in the world, 'for the excellent Example which *Amelia* here gives to all Mothers' (IV, 3). She is also an exemplary wife, as numerous instances testify. Fielding's defence of marriage is less explicit, if only because it occurs first in Booth's account of the great happiness he found in married life, when one delightfully tranquil day was indistinguishable from the next. Representing the scornful, Miss Mathews interposes: '"The dullest of all Ideas."' But Booth continues:

I know . . . it must appear dull in Description; for who can describe the Pleasures which the Morning Air gives to one in Perfect Health; the Flow of Spirits which springs up from Exercise; the Delights which Parents feel from the Prattle, and innocent Follies of their Children; the Joy with which the tender Smile of a Wife inspires a Husband; or lastly, the chearful, solid Comfort which a fond Couple enjoy in each other's Conversation. (III, 12)

None would doubt that Sophia or Fanny is virtuous, but Fielding got his point across before without resorting to such extremely sentimental defence. Although he promoted the cause of virtue in *Tom Jones* and *Joseph Andrews*, his undercutting irony ultimately compromised his position in these novels by making concessions to his readers' scorn.

In *Amelia* Fielding makes no such concessions, yet without sacrificing his customary irony altogether. For instance, near the end, Amelia sweeps past the bailiff's wife, telling her she must see her imprisoned husband. Reunited, they embrace 'for a considerable Time with so much Rapture, that the Bailiff's Wife, who was an Eye-witness of this violent Fondness, began to suspect whether *Amelia* had really told her Truth' (XII, 2). This touch of humorous irony serves to satirise mildly a common conception of marriage and its related social convention. The scene also 'promote[s] the Cause of Virtue', since Booth asks Amelia's forgiveness for his extra-marital transgressions, and, so far from upbraiding him, she says she has nothing to forgive him for. Here, then, is a simple defence of that unfashionable thing, marital love. This is a specific example of the general problem articulated by Dr Harrison, echoing Pope's expression of fourteen years earlier, 'Not to be corrupted is the shame':

I am very sorry . . . to find the Age is grown to so scandalous a Degree of Licentiousness; that we have thrown off not only Virtue, but Decency. How abandoned must be the Manners of any Nation where such Insults upon Religion and Morality can be committed with Impunity? (X, 4)

Fielding seems to be making a last-ditch stand in defence of virtue in a hostile, morally topsy-turvy world.

Virtue may need defending, but it is not feeble. Amelia does not always conform to Thackeray's picture of a milksop unable to do anything except burst into tears at a moment's notice. Like Thackeray, most critics seem inclined to think Amelia at her most typical when 'a Torrent of contending Passions . . . overpowered her gentle Spirits, and she fainted away in [Booth's] Arms' at the end of a scene in which 'the Tears streamed from her bright Eyes' (II, 2). More than once she totters (IV, 7; XII, 2), scarce able to support herself, and when she hears that Booth has been arrested again she 'gave a full Vent to a Passion almost too strong for her delicate Constitution' (VIII, 3). Such delicacy is unthinkable of the robust Fanny or even Sophia. But Amelia's constitution is not always so delicate. When she and Booth attempt to elope by moonlight in a rainstorm, she is tough enough to clamber over hedges and ditches, 'performing the Part of a Heroine all the Way'; then having 'declared herself under no Apprehension of catching Cold', she accepts the old cottager's offer of dry clothes, but reluctantly. Booth adds that 'she hath indeed the best Constitution in the World' (II, 6). So we have conflicting information. Amelia has a delicate constitution when under emotional stress, a robust one when she bestirs herself to action. Despite a certain psychological plausibility, the inconsistency may be due to Fielding's awkward inclusion of the materials of romance, a point on which Sheridan Baker has helpfully commented ('*Amelia* and the Materials of Romance'). The midnight elopement is a standard feature of romance, and although Booth lifts Amelia over a gate, she is too spirited to need carrying all the way. Amelia's constitution also points towards a conception of sentimental character (to which I shall return): she must seem frail enough to be vulnerable to the predatory libertine, but be strong enough, physically and mentally, to resist him.

Amelia, then, is not passive, like Fanny, in having to rely on male support to get her out of a tight spot, although it occasionally happens (for example, IV, 7). Her virtue is not passive either, like that of the Heartfrees. Amelia is at least guarded, even though she can be thoroughly taken in by appearances and therefore put misplaced trust in the noble lord and Colonel James. But where the rest of the social world around her is pretentious, devious, and hypocritical, Amelia is honest and, as Dr Harrison says, entirely without guile (IX, 8). Hers is active virtue.

Because Fielding so often plays down his habitual irony, virtue in *Amelia* is a serious business, a point that is exemplified by comparing the characters of Dr Harrison and Parson Adams. Harrison's role

AMELIA

in relation to Booth and Amelia is equivalent to Adams' protection
of Joseph and Fanny. An exemplary man of unbending Christian
principle, Harrison is admirably virtuous, but he is no figure of fun;
on the contrary, he seems too solemn for words, without any of
Adams' endearing inconsistencies and weaknesses. Fiercely
virtuous, Adams is larger than life, and as such scarcely credible as
a real human being, but Harrison, as incredible as Amelia in his
saintliness, seems otherwise more ordinary and plausible.

Although Fielding does not maintain such radical differences in
the secondary characters, his emphasis has changed in them, too. In
keeping with his established practice, Fielding encapsulates Major
Bath's ridiculousness in a comic caricature that indicates his
ludicrous appearance and his limited conversation: he is ' "a very
aukward thin Man near seven Foot high" ' whom we first encounter
' "having on a Woman's Bed-Gown, and a very dirty Flannel
Night-Cap" '. His oddity, says Booth, ' "might have formed, in the
Opinion of most Men, a very proper Object of Laughter" ', so we
may expect Booth's opinion to have been somehow different. Booth
does laugh, but not at Bath's appearance:

'I would not have you think, Mr. *Booth*, because you have caught me in this
Dishabille, . . . that I am my Sister's Nurse. I know better what is due to the
Dignity of a Man, and I have shewn it in a Line of Battle. – I think I have
made a figure there, Mr. *Booth*, and becoming my Character; by G— I
ought not to be despised too much, if my Nature is not totally without its
Weaknesses.' He utter'd this [continues Booth], and some more of the
same kind, with great Majesty, or as he call'd it, Dignity . . . I could not
easily refrain from Laughter; however, I conquered myself, and soon after
retired from him, astonished that it was possible for a man to possess true
Goodness, and be, at the same time, ashamed of it.   (III, 8)

This is not caricature designed only for laughter, but, rather like the
picture of Blear-Eyed Moll (though far less shocking), a sketch that
makes an unexpected point. Bath's incongruous dignity and his
awkward shame at being caught doing good establish Fielding's
purpose. We know now that he is good-natured, but we also know
that at least one good-natured man prefers to conform publicly to
the behaviour society expects of him, and therefore conceal his
goodness. Similarly, ' "his Discourse generally turned on Matters
of no feminine Kind, War and martial Exploits being the ordinary
Topics of his Conversation," ' reports Booth. Amelia quickly
realises that Bath ' "tells us of many Things which he hath never
seen, and of others which he hath never done, and both in the most

123

extravagant Excess'''', yet Booth recounts her sentiment to expose not Bath's ridiculousness but Amelia's good nature (III, 8).

Among the other prominent secondary characters, the faded beauty, Mrs Atkinson, is mildly ridiculed for her classical learning and her liking for a drop of cherry brandy, but her good nature redeems her. The story of her life, placed symmetrically to match that of Fanny Mathews, is a cautionary tale for her new friend Amelia (VII, 1–9). The two stories contain several parallels, not least the floods of tears which give vent to overwhelming passion at various affecting moments in the narratives. These (of course) induce sympathetic tears from the good-natured and well-bred listeners, Booth in the one case, Amelia in the other. It is worth noting that Fielding expects his readers to respond similarly (IX, 1). Both Miss Mathews and Mrs Atkinson are sturdy survivors, but in quite different ways: Miss Mathews is proudly defiant, considering revenge – in the form of murder – a suitable response to the cynical exploitation to which her shiftless lover subjected her. She survives by becoming just as cynical herself. Mrs Atkinson too has been a victim of sexual exploitation. Though experience has taught her to be pragmatic, Mrs Atkinson is too good-natured to be cynical. Her entrapment by the 'wicked Lord' is about to be re-enacted, with Amelia 'the destined Sacrifice' (VII, 9).

The noble lord is certainly dangerous because his lust is protected by wealth and power, but he is drawn too indistinctly to approach the near-Satanic evil of Blifil. We have little idea of what he looks like, most of his conversation is reported, not direct, and we never even learn his name. As a satiric caricature he is representative of a social type, the aristocratic libertine. If we think just for a moment of Richardson's Lovelace, it is obvious that Fielding endows his lord with very little presence and scarcely attempts to develop the character or investigate the psychology of his libertinism. Fielding does not concentrate on the interaction between two such interesting psyches as Lovelace and Clarissa, but on how Amelia and Booth can evade a series of threats that are emblematic of the cynical society that generates them.

Fielding's other characters also symbolise society, at several levels, in almost all its aspects from the affected to the menacing. For instance, Mrs James (Bath's sister) is merely pretentious, and so really harmless. As soon as she is married, she adopts a new mode of conduct, consistent with 'the great Alteration in her Circumstances, from a State of Dependency on a Brother, who was himself no better than a Soldier of Fortune, to that of being a Wife to a Man of a very large Estate, and considerable Rank in Life' (IV, 6). She has now become 'a fine Lady, who considered Form and Show as essential Ingredients of human Happiness, and imagined all Friendship to consist in Ceremony, Curt'sies, Messages, and Visits' (IV, 6), which eventually provokes in Amelia 'some little unavoidable Contempt' (V, 4). Thus, despite an invitation, Amelia is refused by Mrs James' maid, because it is fashionable sometimes for a 'fine Lady' to affect not to be at home (IV, 6). This perplexes Amelia, who is too ignorant of the ways of the fashionable world to understand how her friend of yesterday can become cold and distant today. Such acquired snobbery as that of Mrs James was ridiculed in *Joseph Andrews*, but even the mildest social satire is mitigated now:

Mrs. *James* now behaved herself so very unlike the Person that she lately appeared, that it might have surprised any one who doth not know, that besides that of a fine Lady, which is all mere Art and Mummery, every such Woman hath some real Character at the Bottom, in which, whenever Nature gets the better of her, she acts. Thus the finest Ladies in the World will sometimes love, and sometimes scratch, according to their different natural Dispositions, with great Fury and Violence, tho' both of these are equally inconsistent with a fine Lady's artificial Character.   (VIII, 9)

Fielding's flat tone guarantees that Mrs James' merely superficial and silly conduct is not censured.

Among the still more minor characters, one of the lord's pimps, Mrs Ellison, is a false comforter in accordance with her role: she is also unaccountably snobbish; Trent, a 'Gentleman' of dubious parentage, having blackmailed the lord, is now scheming with him to ensnare Booth and Amelia, and therefore seems to be generous when he is really setting a trap with the lord's money. Distinctions of social rank certainly have no corresponding moral significance once collaborations like these exist.

Booth and Amelia keep falling into such traps because they cannot penetrate these false appearances: indeed, nobody can, but some people flourish because they assume that everyone else is motivated by the same cynical impulses as they are themselves. As Booth falls into each trap, of his own or someone else's making, the cycle of debt, arrest, and imprisonment begins again. By the end, he must have stopped trusting appearances, but there is no moment of realisation. Learning not to trust appearances is particularly difficult, for although there is a constant tension between the good, or generous, and the evil, or greedy, evil people often seem generous – usually because they are rich and use their wealth as a means of bribery. False generosity is exemplified by the lord, James, and Trent. True generosity is practically personified by Atkinson, the most good-natured and, after Amelia, the most sentimental character in the novel. The problem for anyone trying to master the Art of Life is to learn how to distinguish the true from the false.

Booth and Amelia are obviously not the only characters who are deceived by appearances, but their misjudgments are the most spectacular (for example, their being taken in by Amelia's sister (II, 8)). Everyone from Thrasher onwards makes at least an assumption about another person's temperament, status, or wealth on the basis of clothing or conduct. Dr Harrison is 'shocked at seeing [villainy] so artfully disguised under the Appearance of so much Virtue' (IX, 5), but even he is satisfied by 'ocular Demonstration' of the alleged extravagance of Booth and Amelia, when in fact he sees 'the little Gold Watch, and all those fine Trinkets with which the noble Lord had presented the Children; and which from the Answers given him by the poor ignorant innocent Girl, he could have no Doubt had been purchased within a few Days by *Amelia*' (IX, 1). Although Harrison's conclusion seems reasonable, he still does not know all the facts and is therefore still basing his judgment on appearance. Even he brings an action against Booth – perhaps the most surprising single incident in the whole novel – on the grounds only of what he has heard, and hires Murphy the corrupt lawyer, of all people, in the process (XII, 5).

One character who is constantly misjudged is Colonel James, because he too uses his money with the appearance of generosity (for example, III, 7). We first hear of him when Booth praises his friendship: James, he says, ' "is undoubtedly one of the pleasantest Companions, and one of the best-natured Men in the World. This worthy Man . . . preserved me from Destruction . . . *Bob James* can never be supposed to act from any Motive of Virtue or Religion; since he constantly laughs at both; and yet his Conduct towards me alone demonstrates a Degree of Goodness, which, perhaps, few of the Votaries of either Virtue or Religion can equal" ' (III, 5).

Booth's view, that good nature is not necessarily associated only with the virtuous or religious, is confirmed later by the narrator. When James gives Booth £30 with promises of £20 more and help towards getting him a commission, the narrator first explains that 'generous he really was to the highest Degree' and then pauses: 'Here, Reader, give me leave to stop a minute, to lament that so few are to be found of this benign Disposition' (IV, 4). But in the next chapter we learn that James 'was a perfect Libertine with regard to Women; that being the principal Blemish in his Character, which otherwise might have deserved much Commendation for Good-nature, Generosity, and Friendship' (IV, 5). It seems contradictory that good nature can be attributed to characters as different as James and Harrison. Already a quality that need not accompany virtue and religion, good nature can now be found also in people whose behaviour is affected: 'Mrs. *James* then was at the Bottom a very good-natured Woman; and the Moment she heard of *Amelia's* Misfortune, was sincerely grieved at it' (VIII, 9). The implied contradiction also makes a reader's judgment more difficult, because we are not always quite sure who is good-natured and who is not. So when James turns out to be anything but good-natured, it looks as if we have something more complex than Booth's misjudging a hypocrite once again. We readers are likely to be as perplexed as Booth and Amelia, since the narrator also appears to have misjudged James, as if he were as limited in his vision and knowledge as Booth. If he does not know who to trust, who does?

The same technique applies to the presentation of Mrs Ellison, who is unattractive to look at, but possessed of 'good Humour and Complaisance' (IV, 7). It is not quite enough to say that her 'goodness' is only Amelia's satisfied interpretation of flattery, for the narrator too calls Mrs Ellison a 'good Woman' (IV, 7), and 'indeed a Woman of most profuse Generosity' (V, 7). Such terms must be qualified, because she reveals that she is a snob and annoys Amelia when she says she is 'not so distressed for want of Company' as to be seen in public with Mrs Bennet (VI, 5). Even Amelia, on hearing of Mrs Ellison's role in the noble lord's seduction of Mrs Bennet, 'now burst forth into some very satirical Invectives against that Lady, and declared she had the Art, as well as the Wickedness, of the Devil himself' (VII, 7). At this point, we are left to wonder whose judgment is right. Is she good or evil? The answer seems to come when Mrs Bennet, now Mrs Atkinson, confronts Mrs Ellison with her machinations as a pimp. Mrs Ellison 'burst out of the Room, and out of the House . . . in a Condition of Mind, to which Fortune without Guilt cannot, I believe, reduce any one . . . in [her] Bosom all was Storm and Tempest; Anger, Revenge, Fear, and Pride, like so many raging Furies, possessed her Mind, and tortured her with Disappointment and Shame' (VIII, 3). In presenting Mrs Ellison in the course of four books, the narrator has again contradicted himself, as if his judgment were as suspect as Amelia's.

A similar pattern occurs with the nameless lord. His 'usual good Nature brought him immediately to aquaint Mr. *Booth*' with news of further promises from a great man. And his lordship's 'particular Address' to Amelia 'now appeared to be rather owing to his perfect good Breeding . . . than from any other Preference' (V, 6). The faintly sarcastic irony of '*usual* good Nature' and 'appeared' emerges only later. When Amelia thinks the lord 'so good-natur'd and so generous' (VI, 1) because he has showered gifts on her children, the narrator adds no hints of his own. Booth, who has heard what he takes to be the truth (it is) from James, demurs. In the next chapter (VI, 2) Amelia is praising the lord for his goodness and benevolence; three chapters later (VI, 5) she misses the heaviest of hints that he is not generous unless he can get something out of it; one more, and she still refuses to believe any adverse criticism of him (VI, 6). Only when Mrs Atkinson's tale (which Amelia does believe) produces a parallel to her own by revealing the lord's scheming towards seduction does Amelia change her mind about him (VII, 6).

All of this indicates a new species of narrative for Fielding. Far from being authoritative, the narrator is so uncertain that he frequently leaves his readers guessing as much as his characters. No one can know anyone else all at once: the true nature of the unattractive characters is gradually revealed to readers as it is gradually revealed to the perceptions of the virtuous characters. In this respect, the narrator is like his characters: his vision is incomplete, so that he too makes errors of judgment, which he adjusts as he goes along. But in his case realism is not sustained, since he has the benefit of hindsight. His contradictions also show that in the 'real' world in which Booth and Amelia move, anyone might turn out to be unreliable, but the good-natured characters make the generous mistake of thinking the best of people until some set of circumstances convinces them to see their error. The only difference between the unreliability of the narrator and that of the evidently ill-natured characters is that the narrator does not seem to have any malicious intent to mislead. The Art of Life, perhaps, is not to be misled in the first place or to learn from experience how to read the signs. The trouble is that there are no reliable signs to read, so the only option left is to be wary. *Amelia* turns on the question of Booth's and, to a lesser extent, Amelia's misperception of what is around them. When even the good-natured can be affected snobs whose conduct is offensive, when even Dr Harrison can make the mistake of judging on insufficient evidence, it is plain that prudence or just basic caution is necessary, since good nature alone is not enough to qualify anyone for survival.

There is a further complication. *Amelia*'s central human relationship is so weak that it often provokes the obvious question; as Pat Rogers puts it, why did Amelia ever marry Booth? (*Henry Fielding*, p. 96). The answer appears to be that because Booth is good-natured, Amelia accepts him for what he is. She says he makes her happy, but we see little actual evidence of it: scenes of domestic bliss do not tell us what she sees in him, how he makes her happy. The structural function of their love is more important than its dubious psychological basis. Their love is placed in constant contrast with others' lust, their innocence with others' guilt, their naivety with others' sophistication, their simplicity with others' deviousness, their few demands with the ambition and avarice that surround them.

Good nature and the art of survival are at odds, because the relationship between Amelia and Booth is its own curse. Despite their much-vaunted generosity and openness of heart, they often go through charades of concealment and misunderstanding instead of saying what they know. Sometimes, Booth prefers to mislead Amelia to protect her from the truth, and she misunderstands his mood (for example, IV, 3). When he contemplates admitting to Amelia his affair with Fanny Mathews, he is too ashamed, 'or to speak, perhaps, more truly, he had too much Pride to confess his Guilt, and preferred the Danger of the highest Inconveniences to the Certainty of being put to the Blush' (IV, 5): Amelia mistakes his mean motive, attributing his strange behaviour to his affection and his desire to protect her (IV, 6). Near the end, Booth learns that Amelia has long had Miss Mathews' incriminating letter (XII, 2), but she said nothing about it because she considered it unimportant.

Yet all this works the other way around, too. Amelia wants to leave Bagillard's house in Montpelier, but fabricates a pretext to tell her husband (VIII, 8). She would prefer not to dine with James, but does not press the point far, because she allows herself a little deceit, 'to avoid giving any Umbrage to her Husband' (IX, 2). In their anxiety not to hurt or disturb each other, they do not always tell the whole truth, and so cause precisely the effect they wish to avoid. Mrs Atkinson's view of deception tells only part of the story: 'happy is the deceived Party between true Lovers, and wretched indeed is the Author of the Deceit' (VII, 8). Once, but only once, Dr Harrison concludes that Amelia has 'acted with great Prudence in concealing this Affair [that is, James' villainy] from [her] Husband' (IX, 5).

The misunderstandings they thus cause one another only compound their everyday problems and are consistent with their habit of judging everything they see on appearances.

IV

Like a passport to material rewards, good nature eventually gets Tom Jones, Joseph and Fanny, and the Heartfrees out of their difficulties. But in *Amelia* good nature alone is no longer an index of virtue. The exemplary characters who promote virtue are not merely good-natured, nor even merely virtuous. They are also sentimental.

Amelia is extremely sentimental in its exploitation of the theme of virtue in distress. Constantly in distress, Booth is neither evil nor vicious, but his weaknesses prevent him from being unequivocally virtuous. The focus of the theme is Amelia herself. Amelia's case, Fielding announces, 'however hard, was not absolutely desperate; for scarce any Condition of Fortune can be so. Art and Industry, Chance and Friends have often relieved the most distrest Circumstances, and converted them into Opulence' (VIII, 3). Amelia and Booth rely more on the latter pair than the former. Honest Atkinson, who has saved a tidy sum but is far from wealthy, relieves Booth's debts with characteristic loyalty and generosity, as does the most charitable character of all, Dr Harrison. Distressed virtue is relieved by such acts of charity, but as the gap between true and false generosity widens, motives finally explain and justify actions. In contrast to the lord, James, or Trent, Atkinson's repeated generosity is truly benevolent because its motive is love.

The proper response to generosity is to weep tears of gratitude (for example, VIII, 6). If this proves hard to stomach, surely the philosophy behind it is even less readily digestible, since *Amelia* posits a world in which the benevolent characters are the continual victims of the predatory, and yet the benevolent come out on top in the end. This is Fielding's fictional means of affirming optimism which is denied by hard social realities, and which the novel's realism does little or nothing to justify. Translated into narrative modes, it is a tension between satire and sentiment. Fielding's satire shows that individual acts of generosity such as Atkinson's are exceptional. Because society at large, like the law it spawns, is fundamentally unjust, most victims of injustice will not usually receive any relief at all. *Amelia* never suggests that society might be changed by continual charity, for the very fact that at the end none of the vicious, corrupt, or affected characters reform their ways is enough to tell us that benevolence makes little headway. Benevolence, then, is a sentimental ideal that only clashes with the reality of poverty, cynicism, exploitation, and injustice. The generous, as Fielding had also pointed out in *Joseph Andrews*, are usually poor (XII, 8).

This is all sentimental in the modern use of the term. The virtuous characters are also sentimental in a more respectable, if more restricted, sense, not associated with insincerity or shallowness. When Booth wishes to praise Amelia, he says: 'with all her Simplicity I assure you she is the most sensible Woman in the World' (II, 2). He does not mean that she is a simpleton who somehow manages to act judiciously, but rather that in contrast to artificial social manipulation and posturing, she is both guileless and capable of feeling. She is therefore a woman of sensibility. This explains, for instance, why Amelia is ready to faint when Mrs Atkinson begins her life-story with the death of her mother: Amelia can identify with the bereaved daughter. This ability to sympathise is a sentimental trait that became increasingly popular – not to say overworked – in fiction later in the eighteenth century.

Amelia's obvious 'man of feeling' is Atkinson. He is innately good-natured (V, 3), benevolent, naturally modest (IV, 7), and bashful enough to be socially awkward (V, 2), like Joseph Andrews. Mrs Bennet, who later marries him, is so impressed by his 'faithful, honest, noble, generous Passion' for Amelia, that she is 'convinced his Mind must possess all the Ingredients of such a Passion; and what are these but true Honour, Goodness, Modesty, Bravery, Tenderness, and, in a Word, every human Virtue' (VII, 10). This high praise is never undermined or contradicted anywhere in the novel.

Atkinson's 'almost unparallel'd Fidelity' (III, 5) to Booth is inspired by devotion to his foster-sister, Amelia. Indeed, 'honest' is a sobriquet that occurs so often it becomes almost a part of Atkinson's name. Yet, in one of the novel's most revealing scenes, Atkinson confesses to Amelia the minor 'crime' of stealing a picture of her (XI, 6; for the theft, III, 3). In the very next chapter, Booth explodes with rage at Betty, the maid who has stolen Amelia's linen. Where the law would recognise no distinction between the two acts of theft, Fielding's judgment of these crimes is determined by their motivation. Betty's crime is breach of trust, whereas Atkinson's is motivated by love so pure that

To say the Truth, without any Injury to her Chastity, that Heart which had stood firm as a Rock to all the Attacks of Title and Equipage, of Finery and Flattery, and which all the Treasures of the Universe could not have purchased, was yet a little softened by the plain, honest, modest, involuntary, delicate, heroic Passion of this poor and humble Swain; for whom, in spite of herself, she felt a momentary Tenderness and Complacence, at which *Booth*, if he had known it, would perhaps have been displeased.   (XI, 6)

This scene is the apotheosis of Atkinson's portrait as a man of virtue: throughout the novel he has stood bail for Booth, and now his true and admirable motive is divulged. He stole the picture not, of course, because it is in a gold frame set with diamonds, but because it portrays Amelia. It is typical of sentimentalism in eighteenth-century fiction that such passion as Atkinson's is doomed to frustration. Fielding goes rather too far, however, for Atkinson is not a 'Swain' at all. Since *Amelia* has none of the satiric incongruity of that 'Newgate pastoral', *The Beggar's Opera*, it is incredibly inappropriate that Fielding drifts into the conventions of pastoral romance, where swains love noble ladies with hopeless passion. The epithet serves only to exaggerate the social distinction between Atkinson and Amelia, which their being raised together has blurred, and which Amelia disdains anyway, whatever Atkinson may say about knowing his place. Fielding's social satire still remains intact: despite Atkinson's low birth, the purity of his 'heroic' passion is a lofty, admirable alternative to the rather sordid lust of the noble lord, whose nobility extends no further than his title.

The picture of Amelia proves to be significant, one of 'the several small and almost imperceptible Links in every Chain of Events by which all the great Actions of the World are produced' (XII, 1). To raise money for bail, Amelia pawns her picture. Robinson, who has never seen her before, happens to be in the pawnbroker's shop at the same time, guesses who she is by seeing the picture, realises that he is responsible for her penury, and repents. Conscience leads him to confess his past crime as accessory to Murphy's forgery of Amelia's mother's will, and his confession enables Amelia to receive her due inheritance.

Like the endings of Fielding's previous novels, the last chapters of *Amelia* summarily dispose of the vicious. In *Amelia*, they all meet an appropriate fate, such as Murphy, who is hanged. Robinson alone 'seemed to reform his Life, and received a small Pension from Booth; after which he returned to vicious Courses, took a Purse on the Highway, was detected and taken, and followed the last Steps of his old Master. So apt are Men, whose Manners have been once thoroughly corrupted, to return, from any Dawn of Amendment, into the dark Paths of Vice' (XII, 9). At least corruption is not innate, but once established, it is evidently irrevocable.

In contrast to the vicious, the virtuous come together in serenity, enjoying one another's company without any intrusions from outsiders. In a pattern that is familiar in eighteenth-century writing, the virtuous retire to the country, away from the corruptions and temptations of London. Booth, indeed, has 'paid all his Debts of Honour; after which, and a Stay of two Days only, he returned into the Country, and hath never since been thirty Miles from home' (XII, 9). This is another version of the 'family of love', an expression Fielding introduced in *The Author's Farce* (I, vii, 9) and used again at the close of *Jonathan Wild* to indicate the Heartfrees (IV, 15). The climax of *Amelia* parallels that of *Wild* – and for that matter *Joseph Andrews* and *Tom Jones* – by rewarding those who are benevolent, loyal, and honest with contentment and peace. Such contented retirement from the bustle of city life carries overtones of a return to the Garden of Eden or perhaps more exactly a renewed Golden Age of innocent bliss among experienced adults. Retirement is in any case an emblem of harmony and stability.

One might ask what these people have learned or proved to earn such a reward. Atkinson miraculously eluded the taint of corruption in his six years in the army (IV, 7), so he must be a deserving case, and Amelia's virtue obviously qualifies her for this retreat to an earthly paradise. She has been practically perfect from the outset, but her husband most certainly has not. Not only is Booth naive (VI, 4), gullible, improvident (III, 12), and vain (II, 2): he is also a downright fool at times. He is so easily led that he can risk losing his own money and £50 he has borrowed while Amelia is saving sixpence in order to survive. He is as extravagant as she is economical; he dines out while she eats nothing.

And yet the contrast is not always this consistent. For all her hypocrisy, Mrs Ellison speaks sound sense when she advises Amelia to stop wailing and bawling about her husband's debts and to do something practical about them (VIII, 3). Although Amelia can be pragmatic, she has too little experience of hard urban life to be street-wise. Nevertheless, on the whole, it is not Amelia but Booth who is directly confronted with the problem of learning the hard way, from experience, and making his own luck rather than continuing to blame Fortune. Tom Jones must learn to acquire that ambiguous quality, prudence; Booth really learns neither prudence nor any other pragmatism. All he does is change his mind on one admittedly important issue, Providence.

Early in the novel, Booth is certain 'that every Man acted merely from the Force of that Passion which was uppermost in his Mind, and could do no otherwise' (I, 3). By the end, he has cured himself of this atheistic doctrine and accepted that the world is constituted according to a providential order. Ironically, this should mean that Fortune, which Booth blames at first, has no real role, nor possibly even existence, yet at the end 'Fortune seems to have made [Booth and Amelia] large Amends for the Tricks she played them in their Youth' (XII, 9). In any event, Booth's conversion seems to be enough in itself. If he is exemplary in the end, he represents no recommendation to Fielding's readers any more than the Heartfrees do. Booth's conversion suggests that *Amelia* is finally an exhortation to virtue and sentiment, as if the problems of the world will then evaporate. But they keep returning, as the novel has shown for page after page, so that Fielding's pat solution can exist only in fiction, not in the life his fiction purports to represent.

Amelia, then, is realistic in the sense that it presents the bleak realities of the seamy side of Georgian city life. Realism is limited and weakened finally by Fielding's optimism. In accordance with this kind of realism, *Amelia* seems to lack structure, instead recounting an almost random sequence of events that are similar to one another. And yet this is one of the strengths of the novel: life – especially in the less salubrious environs of central London – is not a rich and varied tapestry, but an altogether more repetitive and more unpleasant affair. And if one owes money, there is little hope of escape from the repeated cycle of menace, arrest, and imprisonment. The very lack of variety in *Amelia* reflects the suffocating world in which Booth and Amelia are forced to live. Forced, that is, until Providence bails them out with the gift of an estate.

6

The Journal of a Voyage to Lisbon

By the end of 1752, Fielding had finished with the *Covent-Garden Journal*. His only other published work in that year was an odd little pamphlet, *Examples of the Interposition of Providence in the Detection and Punishment of Murder*, in which he seemed to profess more faith in miracles than in incompetent law enforcement officers. With his blind half-brother John, but without much help from Providence, Fielding was beginning to organise London's first true police force. In February 1750 they had also opened the Universal Register Office, which functioned as a kind of information exchange and employment agency.

Fielding's mind was now engaged almost solely with legal and social matters. Early in 1753, at the Duke of Newcastle's demand, at four days' notice and in declining health, Fielding managed to write his famous *Proposal for Making an Effectual Provision for the Poor*, a subject he had been mulling over for about two years. In *Amelia* Fielding had blamed maladministration of the law for the dreadful social problems associated with widespread poverty, but in the *Proposal* he advocated reform of the laws themselves. It is hard now to gain a true perspective on Fielding's proposals. Malvin R. Zirker has argued that the legislation Fielding envisaged was repressive, even inhumane, because he sought to exploit the poor by making them work more – for the benefit of the nation as a whole. But one should set against that Fielding's judgments from the bench, which were often anything but repressive: if he thought there was any chance that criminals might reform, he declined to commit them to Newgate or Bridewell, where, as *Amelia* shows, the problem would be exacerbated, and he let them off with a mere admonition.

Fielding's only other work of any serious consequence after *Amelia* was *The Journal of a Voyage to Lisbon*, which he wrote on board ship in the summer of 1754, possibly just to fill his time. His health had been deteriorating so fast that in only a year he had become emaciated, jaundiced, gouty, and asthmatic; he was also suffering from a distended abdomen and such weakness in his legs that he had to be lifted and carried in a chair. In these circumstances Fielding had had to retire from his magistracy, but he still found the energy to revise *Jonathan Wild* for a new edition, which Millar published on 19

March 1754. Fielding also embarked on a refutation of Lord Bolingbroke's philosophical works, which had been published on 6 March, but he died before he could finish this project. The few pages he had written were tacked on to the text of his *Journal of a Voyage to Lisbon*.

In search of a warmer climate, Fielding began his journey on 26 June and kept a journal until his arrival in Lisbon on 6 August, though his dating goes haywire after 13 July. His health improved in Portugal, but he died – suddenly, it seems – on 8 October. Two editions of his *Journal* were published posthumously in 1755. The one that was printed second was published first, on 25 February. It is a shortened version, somewhat carelessly printed. The version that had been printed first became the second edition, published in early December. This longer text, which I quote here, is thought to be an unedited printing of Fielding's manuscript, which has not survived.

Each edition begins with an almost patronising 'Dedication to the Public' written either by Millar or, more probably, by Fielding's later editor, Arthur Murphy. The dedicator likened Fielding to 'a lamp almost burnt out', which flickers rather than blazes (pp. i–ii; Everyman, 181). Not, one would think, a promising advertisement for a book calculated (in spite of its untranslated Latin quotations) to be popular enough to raise money for Fielding's family. The dedicator goes on: 'if in this little work there should appear any traces of a weaken'd and decay'd life, let your own imaginations place before your eyes a true picture, in that of a hand trembling in almost its latest hour, of a body emaciated with pains, yet struggling for your entertainment; and let this affecting picture open each tender heart, and call forth a melting tear' (ii; Ev. 181). But the *Journal* is not the work of an enfeebled mind, as this sentimental appeal implies. Uneven though it is, the *Journal* contains sharp observations of character, some satirical protest, and fascinating glimpses of Fielding himself, all mediated by a human warmth that makes the book memorable and valuable.

Fielding must have been one of those people to whom extraordinary things happen. Having determined on Lisbon, he found himself on a ship captained by a penny-pinching, seventy-year-old ex-pirate who believed in witchcraft. The ship, the *Queen of Portugal*, lay windbound on the Thames and then on the south coast of England for much of the time covered by the *Journal*, giving Fielding the time and leisure to depict two such bizarre people (whose names vary in the two editions) as the innkeeper and her husband at Ryde on the Isle of Wight. These two, who would have been in place in any of his novels, suggest that perhaps the comic characters of his fiction came, with little exaggeration, straight from life. Indeed, Richardson had denigrated Fielding before for having 'little or no invention', instead drawing continually on his own experience and merely portraying himself, his wife, and his friends as fictional characters (*Correspondence*, IV, 60–1). More generally, the *Journal* contains several brief protests about parsimony, overcharging, luxury, vanity, inhumanity, and injustice, all of which arise directly from Fielding's experiences.

The statement of his purpose, to convey 'entertainment and information' (Preface, p. [i]; Ev. 183), is merely conventional, but Fielding also tells us that travel literature is a form of history and his *Journal* a record of truth. We have heard that one before, from such 'reliable' historians as Defoe, Swift, and any number of travel writers. One unconvincing suggestion has been made that the *Journal* parodies travel literature by digressing on trivial subjects. Fielding's playful comments about truth and history are close enough to his remarks in his novels about himself as 'historian' to indicate satiric intent, but he aims at social ills, not writers of travel books. He protests too much when he contrasts the *Odyssey* with his modest journal: 'in reality, the Odyssy [*sic*], the Telemachus, and all of that kind, are to the voyage-writing I here intend, what romance is to true history, the former being the confounder and corrupter of the latter' (Preface, vii; Ev. 185). I doubt if this means that Fielding was genuinely repudiating fiction (which would be surprising), because the *Journal* uses techniques that overlap unmistakably with his fictional methods. Before insisting once more that he writes not romance but truth, Fielding admits that 'Some few embellishments must be allowed to every historian' (Preface, xiii; Ev. 188), so that for example dialogues are not recorded verbatim, but reconstituted or reimagined. The *Journal* is less objective than it seems, partly because Fielding toys with his readers again, only this time he speaks through a sentimental persona who sounds personal and honest enough to be the author.

The beginning of the journal proper (after the introduction) shows Fielding in a sentimental role like Booth, really, overcome by emotion when he parts from his children. His wife, like Amelia, 'behaved more like a heroine and philosopher, tho' at the same time the tenderest mother in the world' (40; Ev. 201). The echo of *Amelia* (II, 6) shows rather that Booth and Amelia are close to reality than that Fielding's portrait of himself and his wife here is fictional. In the introduction, with the aggressively bare rhetoric of a political pamphlet, Fielding has already defended himself against the suspicion that he lined his pockets during his magistracy. We encounter him like this, as he wishes to be perceived, often enough to suppose that his self-portrait is not objective (how could it be?) but not idealised, either. Certainly, his pleasures are the same as those of Jones and Booth, especially conversation, without which he is a fish out of water. The note of disappointment when he is deprived of company is surely personal: tormented by toothache, his wife has finally gone to bed, exhausted,

a circumstance which would have given me some happiness, could I have known how to employ those spirits which were raised by it: but unfortunately for me, I was left in a disposition of enjoying an agreeable hour, without the assistance of a companion, which has always appeared to me necessary to such enjoyment . . .   (76; Ev. 218)

Here we can see the gregarious man on whom perhaps all the narrators were based, from *The Champion* to *Amelia*.

We are never in doubt about Fielding's opinions. Always making his presence felt, he is equally at home sounding off about the customs officials having too many holidays or reprimanding a riding-surveyor of the Customs house who barges in unannounced and wears his hat in front of a lady (41, 70–1; Ev. 201, 215–16). The *Journal* is suffused with Fielding's opinions and judgments, yet it is autobiographical only in a limited way. Its principal purpose is plainly to record the interesting things that happened to its author and his reflections on them, not to reveal or portray himself: there is nothing confessional about his narrative. Hence we know Fielding's own response when he describes

the disagreeable situation in which we then lay, in the confines of Wapping and Redriffe [an old name for Rotherhithe], tasting a delicious mixture of the air of both these sweet places, and enjoying the concord of sweet sounds of seamen, watermen, fish-women, oyster-women, and of all the vociferous inhabitants of both shores, composing altogether a greater variety of harmony than Hogarth's imagination hath brought together in that print of his, which is enough to make a man deaf to look at . . .   (44–5; Ev. 203)

Although this may suggest a touch of the snob, whatever we learn about Fielding himself is outweighed by the colourful, crowded, noisy, and unpleasant scene he evokes, with a typically assured appeal to a familiar analogue, Hogarth's *Enraged Musician*.

Fielding is at his best when describing the rude official or Captain Veal or Mrs Francis (called Mrs Humphrys in the shorter text) the innkeeper. The riding-surveyor wore the offending hat 'cocked with much military fierceness on his head' (69; Ev. 215), in a manner reminiscent of Jonathan Wild (II, 4). After being told off, he 'took his covering from his head, and laid it on the table, saying, he asked pardon, and blamed the mate, who, he said, should have informed him if any persons of distinction were below' (70; Ev. 216). Fielding then tells him, 'that as he seemed sensible of his error, and asked pardon, the lady would permit him to put his hat on again, if he chose it': duly humiliated, the man rejects such condescension 'with some degree of surliness, and failed not to convince me that, if I should condescend to become more gentle, he would soon grow more rude' (71; Ev. 216). This passage is less notable for Fielding's inventiveness in the description, or even for the glimpse we catch of his hauteur, than for the sure sense of see-sawing human interaction, nicely caught by the counterpointed phrasing of the last sentence. Surely, too, we have all experienced truculent minor officials who throw their weight about (even if we do not tell them to mind their manners).

In a pattern characteristic of the *Journal*, Fielding uses this rather minor incident as a starting point for a digression on the abuse of power, first in broad political terms, then in the specific case of petty officials. The tyranny of those who, in Fielding's view, should be serving the public is a repeated motif of the *Journal*. He objects to the stage-coachman and the sea captain, who disrupt the passenger's schedule by choosing their own (50, 54; Ev. 206–8), the ferryboatmen who charge exorbitant fees because they know they have a captive market (80–1, 152–3; Ev. 220, 254), and assorted tradesmen, innkeepers, and servants who care nothing for their customers' wishes but willingly take their money (95; Ev. 227). These are all familiar complaints from Fielding' novels – usually from the narrator, who uses specific incidents as examples of the general case – but now the protests enter more serious territory. As he is eating excellent fish in Devon, Fielding wonders why London's poor cannot live on such nutritious and cheap food. The depressing reason is that fish has been made a fashionable luxury in the capital, and therefore its price is held as high as possible. Starvation is thus perpetuated by a whim of the idle rich (170–3; Ev. 262–3), who are censured also because they scoff at the devotion of churchgoers (198; Ev. 276).

While Fielding's journey (unlike Cibber's life) was not

undertaken only so that he could write about it, his experiences have the flavour of examples on which he may base generalisations. Examples such as these could suggest that the *Journal* is an outspoken protest against social evils, yet these serious protests are more like the by-products of Fielding's experience of human nature, and are expressed without the intensity or anger of his social pamphlets and, in places, *Amelia*. The point is easily made by looking at the most memorable character in the *Journal*, Mrs Francis. Her husband 'left the [inn] entirely to the care of his wife, and he acted wisely, I believe, in so doing' (106; Ev. 232), for she is his complementary opposite, vinegar to his oil (112; Ev. 235), a domineering wife with a mousy husband. Fielding caricatures her as an example of 'nature', which

is seldom curious in her works within; without employing some little pains on the outside; and this more particularly in mischievous characters . . . A tyrant, a trickster, and a bully, generally wear the marks of their several dispositions in their countenances; so do the vixen, the shrew, the scold, and all other females of the like kind.

Such an observation might have lurked behind Fielding's conception of Mrs Tow-wouse or Blear-Eyed Moll, but not Blifil, Mrs Ellison, nor the noble lord who tries to seduce Amelia. Fielding goes on:

But, perhaps, nature had never afforded a stronger example of all this, than in the case of Mrs. Francis. She was a short, squat woman; her head was closely joined to her shoulders, where it was fixed somewhat awry; every feature of her countenance was sharp and pointed; her face was furrowed with the small-pox; and her complexion, which seemed to be able to turn milk to curds, not a little resembled in colour such milk as had already undergone that operation. (113; Ev. 235–6)

And, to cap it all, she has a loud, penetrating voice, which woke Fielding every morning and usually 'entertained' him throughout the day (114; Ev. 236). The equivalent portrait in his fiction, that of Mrs Tow-wouse, led Fielding to make a satirical association between her ugly appearance and her unpleasant conduct. But despite some resemblances, Mrs Francis is not exposed to the full force of satiric ridicule. When he does condemn her, he does so gently.

This parsimonious woman gets everything the wrong way round: she neither lights a fire nor prepares the Fieldings' food, because she is more interested in making her house look right for 'gentlefolks' than in seeing to their needs or wishes. She is scandalised when they prefer to eat in a barn rather than a cold dining-room. Her bills, which go up every day, are proportioned like those of Fielding's other landladies and innkeepers to what she thinks she can get, not to what the 'very bad ale . . . rusty bacon and worse cheese' (107; Ev. 233) are worth. Annoyed, but not enraged at such transparent fleecing, Fielding disputes her bill, to make his point, and then pays it (105; Ev. 232). When he later calls her daily charges a tax, he is joking: his good humour is much in evidence, as it seems he is more fascinated than irritated by the lengths to which her ingenuity will go to find something new to add to the bill.

Fielding's playful good humour is more in keeping with his early novels than his last one. While the pleasure of eating heartily in a barn recalls Amelia's repeated preference of a cottage to a palace, it also recalls the travellers in *Joseph Andrews* who prefer robust fare to the 'elegance' which is associated with the ambiguous manners of delicate diners in St James's (100–1; Ev. 230; *Joseph Andrews*, II, 16). In a tone and manner consistent with the endings of all his novels, Fielding prefers to delight in simple pleasures than expend his energy condemning the more fashionable ones. The *Journal* generally shows Fielding in good humour despite appalling ill health, 'curious' rather than slighted when sailors laugh and joke at his expense because in his illness he cuts such a ghastly figure (42–3; Ev. 202–3). Although he recognises their malevolence, he writes of it coolly, with more interest than indignation. Knowing that people do not often change their attitudes, he prefers to accept them as they are. A slightly amused, distanced yet not entirely detached tone seems to be Fielding's natural voice.

There is much of Fielding's own personality, or what we know of it, in both his fiction and his *Journal*. A convivial man who enjoyed company made his likeable characters such as Adams and Jones thrive on conversation over a bottle. Booth and Jones are noticeably depressed not only in prison, but anywhere they feel alone. Fielding himself would have enjoyed the cosy communities in which he cocoons his virtuous characters at the end of each novel. He also knew at first hand the dreadful spectre of debt: perhaps only those who did, like himself and Defoe, could convey the debtor's despair in an uncharitable world. Debts seem easier to cope with when we have to deal with bank managers, not prisons. Fielding's writing also conveys a strong sense of the pleasure of benevolence: giving, relieving distress, helping to take a weight off someone's shoulders (and mind) by paying their bills. This is stronger than his sense of indignation or mere disappointment that so many people who can easily afford it refuse to part with a penny to help anyone except themselves. More often than not, Fielding does not vigorously condemn such people, nor subject them to punitive satire, but dismisses them as small-minded, silly, or otherwise beneath his notice (for example, *Journal*, 108; Ev. 233). His characteristic mode is satiric, but he is more observer than reformer. Because his comedy stresses his fascination with the vagaries of human nature, his satire lacks that commitment to punish or destroy which Pope or Swift often take upon themselves. This does not mean that Fielding was a half-hearted satirist overcome by smug optimism, but that he places more emphasis on attractive alternatives, devoting more energy to celebrating good nature and good humour than to excoriating vice.

In the 1980s readers probably derive more pleasure from Fielding's controlled structures, his conscious artifice, in short his technique, than from his creation of exemplary characters or his optimistic expression of benevolence. But Fielding's narratives have also been condemned because they are tightly contrived, presided over by a didact, peopled by characters too symbolic to be more than ciphers in plots so implausible that readers can admire the structure at a distance, but scarcely respond to any recognisable human emotion. Yet, affective or not, all his fiction expresses a thoroughly human logic of concupiscence: his major male characters, and some minor female ones, are motivated by sexual desire, sometimes repressed by thoughts of chastity, sometimes openly violent and ugly. *Jonathan Wild*, *Joseph Andrews*, and *Tom Jones* depend on the authority of the intrusive narrator for the expression of this logic, as they do for their ironic effects, and indeed for most of their comedy and satire, since their point would be lost if readers read subtext for text. Thus the narrator unequivocally guides his assumed readers, to ensure that ironies, observations, and jokes are shared. Although this sometimes makes Fielding's humour seem ponderous, the social role of the intrusive narrator is crucial if the moral themes of his comic romances are to appear unambiguous and not be susceptible to misunderstanding. *Amelia*, however, decentres such assumed reading by undermining the traditional authority of the author and, unlike Fielding's other fiction, *Amelia* is neither particularly good-humoured nor very funny, which may be enough to explain its relative unpopularity. Few, perhaps, would deny the appeal of Fielding's usual good humour, but to admire it apparently involves the heretical risk of condemning Fielding to the level of a 'Jolly Good Read' to take on a long train journey. His best writing certainly satisfies one important human need, the need to laugh.

Select bibliography

For full listings of primary and secondary materials published up to 1968, see *The New Cambridge Bibliography of English Literature* II (Cambridge: University Press, 1971), 925–48. For blandly annotated lists, mainly of Fielding criticism, John A. Stoler and Richard D. Fulton, *Henry Fielding: An Annotated Bibliography of Twentieth-Century Criticism, 1900–1977* (New York and London: Garland, 1980) is useful despite all its misprints. Best for concise critical listings of Fielding criticism is H. George Hahn, *Henry Fielding: An Annotated Bibliography*, Scarecrow Author Bibliographies No. 41 (Metuchen, N.J., and London: Scarecrow, 1979).

I. Fielding's works

The Complete Works of Henry Fielding, Esq. Ed. William Ernest Henley. 16 vols. 1903; reprinted, New York: Barnes & Noble, 1967.

Amelia. Ed. Martin C. Battestin. Wesleyan edition. Oxford: Clarendon Press, 1983. Standard, with excellent notes.

The Author's Farce. Ed. Charles B. Woods. Regents Restoration Drama Series. Lincoln: University of Nebraska Press, 1966. Original version, not the later revision. Good notes.

The Covent-Garden Journal. Ed. Gerard E. Jensen. 2 vols. New Haven: Yale University Press, 1915. Until Bertrand A. Goldgar's edition appears in the Wesleyan series, this will have to do.

The Covent Garden Tragedy. In *Burlesque Plays of the Eighteenth Century*, ed. Simon Trussler. London: Oxford University Press, 1969, pp. 171–208. Reprint, without notes.

The Grub-Street Opera. Ed. Edgar V. Roberts. Regents Restoration Drama Series. Lincoln· University of Nebraska Press, 1968. Good notes. There is also an edition by L. J. Morrissey (Edinburgh: Oliver & Boyd, 1973).

The Historical Register for the Year 1736 and Eurydice Hiss'd. Ed. William W. Appleton. Regents Restoration Drama Series. Lincoln: University of Nebraska Press, 1967. Provides useful context of theatrical history and the Licensing Act, but no comment on *Eurydice Hiss'd*.

The Jacobite's Journal and Related Writings. Ed. W. B. Coley. Wesleyan edition. Oxford: Clarendon Press, 1975. Standard. The related writings are three political pamphlets from 1747–8.

Jonathan Wild. Ed. David Nokes. Harmondsworth: Penguin, 1982. Best text, best notes, many of which duplicate Brooks' annotation (see below). An added bonus is Defoe's life of Wild.

Jonathan Wild and *The Journal of a Voyage to Lisbon*. Introduction by A. R. Humphreys, notes by Douglas Brooks. Everyman's Library. London: Dent, and New York: Dutton, 1973. Reprints the 1754 text of *Wild* and the 2nd edition (December 1755) of the *Journal*. Useful notes.

Joseph Andrews. Ed. Martin C. Battestin. Wesleyan edition. Oxford: Clarendon Press, 1967. Standard. The same text, with even more extensive notes and a lucid, concise introduction, is accompanied by *Shamela* in Battestin's Riverside edition (Boston: Houghton Mifflin, 1961). There is also a good Penguin edition, ed. R. T. Brissenden (1977). Maynard Mack's Rinehart edition (New York: Holt, 1948) has a valuable introduction, reprinted in Paulson, *Fielding* (see below). *Joseph Andrews and Shamela*, ed. Douglas Brooks (London: Oxford University Press, 1970), has reliable texts and concise notes.

A Journey from this World to the Next. Introduction by Claude Rawson. Everyman's Library. London: Dent, and New York: Dutton, 1973. Reprints the text from *Miscellanies*, 1743. Excellent, brief introduction.

Miscellanies by Henry Fielding, Esq. Vol. 1. Ed. Henry Knight Miller. Wesleyan edition. Oxford: Clarendon Press, 1972. Very full, helpful notes.

Pasquin. Ed. O. M. Brack, Jr, William Kupersmith, and Curt Zimansky. Iowa City: University of Iowa Press, 1973.

An Apology for the Life of Mrs Shamela Andrews. Introduction by Ian Watt. Augustan Reprint Society, no. 57. Los Angeles: William Andrews Clark Memorial Library, 1956. Facsimile reprint of the first edition. For other editions, see also under *Joseph Andrews*, above.

The History of Tom Jones, A Foundling. Introduction and notes by Martin C. Battestin, text edited by Fredson Bowers. 2 vols. Wesleyan edition. Oxford: Clarendon Press, 1974. The paperback (New York: Columbia University Press, 1975) corrects some errors and is therefore the better text, whose authority no other edition approaches. The notes are enormously helpful.

Tom Thumb and the Tragedy of Tragedies. Ed. L. J. Morrissey. Fountainwell Drama Texts 14. Edinburgh: Oliver & Boyd; Berkeley and Los Angeles: University of California Press, 1970. The 1730 version and the 1731 revision, with a handy introduction. The 3rd edition exists in a facsimile reprint (Menston: Scolar Press, 1973).

The True Patriot: and The History of Our Own Times. Ed. Miriam Austin Locke. [Tuscaloosa, Ala.:] University of Alabama Press, 1964. Facsimile reprint with commentary on each essay.

'New Verse by Henry Fielding'. Ed. Isobel M. Grundy. *PMLA* 87(1972), 213–45. Transcript of Fielding's MS (circa 1729 and 1733), with ample notes.

SELECT BIBLIOGRAPHY

II. Biographical sources

Battestin, M. C., and R. R. Battestin. 'Fielding, Bedford, and the Westminster Election of 1749'. *Eighteenth-Century Studies* 11 (1977–8), 143–85. On Bedford's patronage of Fielding, with relevant correspondence.

Cross, Wilbur L. *The History of Henry Fielding*. 3 vols. New Haven: Yale University Press, 1918. Until Martin C. and Ruthe Battestin's biography is completed, Cross remains standard.

Richardson, Samuel. *Correspondence*. Ed. Anna Laetitia Barbauld. 6 vols. London: Richard Phillips, 1804.

Rogers, Pat. *Henry Fielding*. London: Paul Elek, and New York: Scribner, 1979. Concise and readable.

III. Major criticism

Alter, Robert. *Fielding and the Nature of the Novel*. Cambridge, Mass.: Harvard University Press, 1968. Art as artifice.

Baker, Sheridan. 'Fielding's *Amelia* and the Materials of Romance'. *Philological Quarterly* 41 (1962), 437–49.

Battestin, Martin C. *The Moral Basis of Fielding's Art: A Study of 'Joseph Andrews'*. Middletown, Conn.: Wesleyan University Press, 1959. Shows Fielding's indebtedness to Latitudinarian Christianity, in particular its doctrine of benevolence.

The Providence of Wit: Aspects of Form in Augustan Literature and the Arts. Oxford: Clarendon Press, 1974. Valuable chapters show that *Tom Jones* is constructed according to the Design Argument and that the novel's main theme is the achievement of wisdom.

Battestin, Martin C., ed. *Twentieth Century Interpretations of 'Tom Jones'*. Englewood Cliffs, N.J.: Prentice-Hall, 1968. Useful essays by Battestin, Andrew Wright, R. S. Crane, and Robert Alter.

Beasley, Jerry C. *Novels of the 1740s*. Athens, Ga: University of Georgia Press, 1982. A survey of fiction, much of it minor, from the decade of Fielding's greatest productivity.

Blanchard, Frederic T. *Fielding the Novelist: A Study in Historical Criticism*. New Haven: Yale University Press, 1926. A thorough survey of critical attitudes to Fielding from his own time to 1925.

Folkenflik, Robert. 'Purpose and Narration in Fielding's *Amelia*'. *Novel* 6 (1973), 168–74. On the absent narrator and the potentially tragic mode of *Amelia*.

Goldgar, Bertrand A. *Walpole and the wits: The Relation of Politics to Literature, 1722–42*. Lincoln and London: University of Nebraska Press, 1976. Charts Fielding's political affiliations, in a time of complex and confusing political relationships.

Harrison, Bernard. *Henry Fielding's 'Tom Jones': The Novelist as Moral Philosopher*. London: Sussex University Press, 1975. Sets *Tom Jones* convincingly in the context of eighteenth-century philosophy.

146

Hatfield, Glenn W. *Henry Fielding and the Language of Irony*. Chicago and London: University of Chicago Press, 1968. The only sensitive study of Fielding's language, which links him especially with Johnson and Pope in associating abuse of language with declining civilisation.

Hilles, Frederick W. 'Art and Artifice in *Tom Jones*' in *Imagined Worlds: Essays on some English Novels and Novelists in Honour of John Butt* (London: Methuen, 1968), 91–110.

Hunter, J. Paul. *Occasional Form: Henry Fielding and the Chains of Circumstance*. Baltimore and London: Johns Hopkins University Press, 1975. Shows that the novels depend as much on contemporary issues as on traditional literary forms.

Irwin, W. R. *The Making of 'Jonathan Wild': A Study in the Literary Method of Henry Fielding*. 1941; reprinted, Hamden, Conn.: Archon Books, 1966. Studies the literary, philosophical and biographical material on which Fielding drew.

Miller, Henry Knight. *Essays on Fielding's 'Miscellanies': A Commentary on Volume One*. Princeton: Princeton University Press, 1961. Major commentary on Fielding's minor writing.

Park, William. 'What Was New About the "New Species of Writing"?' *Studies in the Novel* 2 (1970), 112–30. What was new was the assimilation by Richardson and Fielding of a diverse mass of fictional materials, which only they organised into integrated, coherent wholes.

Paulson, Ronald. *Fielding: A Collection of Critical Essays*. Twentieth Century Views. Englewood Cliffs, N.J.: Prentice-Hall, 1962. Useful collection.

'Fielding in *Tom Jones*: the Historian, the Poet, and the Mythologist' in *Augustan Worlds: Essays in Honour of A. R. Hunphreys*, ed. J. C. Hilson, M. M. B. Jones, and J. R. Watson (Leicester: Leicester University Press, 1978), 175–88.

Paulson, Ronald, and Thomas F. Lockwood. *Henry Fielding: The Critical Heritage*. London: Routledge & Kegan Paul, 1969. Valuable collection of eighteenth-century opinions about Fielding, with an incisive introduction.

Preston, John. *The Created Self: The Reader's Role in Eighteenth-Century Fiction*. London: Heinemann, 1970. How Fielding teaches his readers to read.

Rawson, C. J. *Henry Fielding and the Augustan Ideal Under Stress: 'Nature's Dance of Death' and other Studies*. London: Routledge & Kegan Paul, 1972. Idiosyncratic, vivid, stimulating, and occasionally brilliant – especially on *Amelia*.

Rothstein, Eric. *Systems of Order and Inquiry in Later Eighteenth-Century Fiction*. Berkeley: University of California Press, 1975. A convincing chapter on *Amelia* (pp. 154–207) uses the inconspicuous narrator to argue that readers and characters acquire knowledge in the same way.

Sherbo, Arthur. *English Sentimental Drama*. East Lansing, Michigan: Michigan State University Press, 1957.

Satire and the Novel in Eighteenth-Century England. New Haven and London: Yale University Press, 1967.

Sherburn, George. 'Fielding's *Amelia*: An Interpretation'. *ELH* 3 (1936), 1–14. Reprinted in Paulson, *Fielding*. Still a valuable essay in rehabilitation.

Wendt, Allan. 'The Moral Allegory of *Jonathan Wild*'. *ELH* 24 (1957), 306–20. Sees *Wild* as an allegory in a context of contemporary ethics.

'The Naked Virtue of Amelia'. *ELH* 27 (1960), 131–48. Amelia – both character and symbol – is the focus of the themes of benevolence, Providence, and virtue.

Work, James A. 'Henry Fielding, Christian Censor'. In *The Age of Johnson: Essays Presented to Chauncey Brewster Tinker*, ed. Frederick W. Hilles. New Haven: Yale University Press, 1949, pp. 139–48. An important essay that uses the *Champion*, mostly, to reveal Fielding's Christianity.

Wright, Andrew. *Henry Fielding: Mask and Feast.* Berkeley: University of California Press, 1965. By stressing the festive role of the fiction, especially through the function of the narrator, Wright argues that the novels are more comic than satiric.

Zirker, Malvin R. *Fielding's Social Pamphlets: A Study of 'An Enquiry into the Causes of the Late Increase of Robbers' and 'A Proposal for Making an Effectual Provision for the Poor'.* Berkeley: University of California Press, 1966. The only study of its kind. Revisionist, reductive, important.

Index

INDEX

INDEX

INDEX